THE OFFICIAL
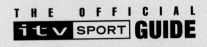 GUIDE

FORMULA ONE

GRAND PRIX >>>>>
2003

THIS IS A CARLTON BOOK
This edition published in 2003
10 9 8 7 6 5 4 3 2 1

A CIP catalogue record for this book is available from
the British Library

The publisher has taken reasonable steps to check the accuracy of the facts contained
herein at the time of going to press but can take no responsibility for any errors

ISBN 1 84222 813 7

Project Editor: Martin Corteel
Editorial Assistant: David Ballheimer
Project Art Direction: Darren Jordan
Cover design: Steve Lynn
Design: Brian Flynn
Production: Lisa French
Picture Research: Marc Glanville

Printed in Italy

Page 7: **Crossing the great divide:**
Former driver, now commentator, Martin
Brundle (left) chats with former driver
and one-time team owner Jackie Stewart.

THE OFFICIAL ITV SPORT GUIDE

FORMULA ONE
GRAND PRIX >>>>>> 2003

BRUCE JONES

CARLTON
BOOKS

≫CONTENTS

Chapter 5

Chapter 6

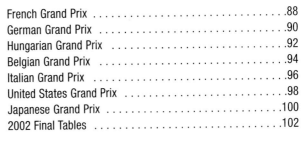

>> FOREWORD

MARTIN BRUNDLE

Without doubt Formula One has been in the wars in the past few months and finally worldwide events have caught up with the highly-fuelled world of Grand Prix spending. We have seen many teams cut back on their budgets and aspirations. One or two have been heading into survival mode. Having said that, most teams will still be spending more money and carrying more team members than, say, three years ago, so everything is relative. However, the sponsors are harder to find and Formula One has lost some of its casual viewers, even if the hard core petrolheads are as loyal as ever.

So what has Formula One done about this? There have been several attempts to cut costs but the bosses of the big-three teams are never going to give away their competitive advantage to others who in their eyes have done a bad job or simply trousered more of their sponsorship money than would have been beneficial to the team. Collectively, the bosses would struggle to agree unanimously on which day of the week it was let alone on a raft of new regulations. This soap opera aspect of Formula One remains fascinating with the handful of real decision-makers jockeying for position in the most cunning and intriguing way.

People say that a change is as good as a rest and with this in mind the qualifying format will be transformed for 2003 with a one-at-a-time format, something that I think is very much a change for the better. I well remember venturing out on to a Grand Prix track with a set of qualifying tyres that were only good for about five miles. That is a cautious out-lap, a manic and scary hot lap, followed by the carefree in-lap to the pit lane, either celebrating or commiserating the effort and lap time just achieved. It is going to be the same in 2003 except all eyes are on the driver for his every turn of the wheel and squeeze of the throttle pedal. At least back then we could sneak out during the qualifying hour in our own time, but now the world's best drivers are going to have to show their skill to us all in real time and in less than two minutes. It is going to be fascinating and it will occasionally make for some exciting grids when driver error, mechanical failure or inclement weather intervenes. That should surely make for better racing.

They have not changed enough for race day itself, but some of the work necessary to fix that problem has been in place since mid-2002 as BMW Williams and McLaren Mercedes-Benz strive to close the gap to Ferrari. That is the purest way of fixing the competition void and let us hope they get it right. Don't be surprised if Ferrari dominate the first few races as they have such a competitive advantage. But the law of diminishing returns must dictate that a car as good as the 2002 Ferrari has less room for improvement than the Williams and McLaren cars. Indeed, on-board cameras showed Michael Schumacher and Rubens Barrichello making very few corrections around the circuit as the car seemed simply glued to the track.

A key element in the closeness of the racing will be whether or not the Michelins can more satisfactorily match the very specialist Bridgestone tyre which suits the Ferrari so well. Let us hope they have done some good work over the winter too.

The middle of the pack will see Renault trying to escape to join the big-three and a furious battle once more between BAR, Jaguar, Jordan, Toyota and Sauber with Minardi keeping a relatively close watch and hopefully embarrassing some of them from time to time. Let's hope they all make the grid in Melbourne.

Be patient until the middle of the season when we can see if the radical new cars from McLaren and Williams have done the job. Also keep a careful watch to see if Montoya can deliver his promise, Coulthard can take his championship or the new kids in town such as Raikkonen, Alonso, Webber and Pizzonia are ready to seize the high ground. Personally I am looking forward to every moment of it.

On last year's form, you'd be a fool to bet against Ferrari staying on top of the pile in 2003. But, in Formula One, you never can quite tell. Williams and McLaren have been shifting heaven and earth to close the deficit that they endured last year. And, with their record of success, regaining the front will only be a matter of when rather than if. Watch on.

There was much beating of the brow last year, with rule proposals by the dozen being considered in an attempt to make Formula One closer. But all talk of success ballast and the like was, rightfully, dismissed. After all, winning in Formula One is surely about being the best. And Ferrari was markedly that last year. As we closed for press, there weas still talk that telemetry and traction control might yet be banned.

With continuity of personnel at Maranello, expect their package to be extremely strong again. Especially with the peerless Michael Schumacher in its lead car and Rubens Barrichello sure to be fast in support.

However, the first clear indication of their comparative speed will come when the cars assemble for the opening Grand Prix in Melbourne. Even then, the issue will be masked, as Williams and McLaren emulate Ferrari in 2002 by keeping their new cars back until the fourth round.

One measure that will undoubtedly improve the show is the reordering of qualifying, with each driver having just one flying lap, held one driver at a time. If pit-to-car radio can be opened up, then we really will have a show like never before.

Williams is certain to up its ante, while McLaren is also hoping for gains, especially from engine supplier Mercedes.

Both teams will be praying that their Michelin rubber is more competitive this year, anxious to close the gap on Bridgestone who enjoyed such supremacy with Ferrari. Pooling their findings could be of great benefit to both teams. It's not just the teams

that will be anxious to start shine, as drivers Juan Pablo Montoya, Ralf Schumacher and David Coulthard are dying to be winners again, while flying Finn Kimi Raikkonen will be out to break his duck.

With money in reduced supply, expect the well-funded works teams from Renault and Toyota to progress in 2003. Renault blew hot and cold in 2002, but Jarno Trulli is capable of delivering a top result when the car's ready, and Fernando Alonso will be champing at the bit to race again after a season on the sidelines. Toyota has more ground to make up. Even with the first chassis from Gustav Brunner, it remains to be seen how new recruits Olivier Panis and CART champion Cristiano da Matta work out.

Sauber could spring a surprise, as they will be running Ferrari's 2002 spec engines and the F2002's trend-setting rear-end. BAR will be hoping that sole use of Honda engines will lead to advancement. Jacques Villeneuve

and new signing Jenson Button will certainly be praying that this will be the case.

Ford expects success, so Jaguar had better advance in 2003 with new signings Mark Webber and Antonio Pizzonia. However, the first shoots of progress emerged in the closing races last year, so there is hope. The engines they used in 2002 will be rebadged as Fords and used by Jordan, with Giancarlo Fisichella sure to prosper if the car is competitive. Minardi will simply be praying to scoop a point or two. However, with the points system being changed to 10-8-6-5-4-3-2-1 for the first eight drivers to the finish, rather than the 10-6-4-3-2-1 system used in 2002, they have more chance than ever.

There has been much talk of cutting costs in recent years, but, as a result of the arrival of hard times last year, the team chiefs are finally listening. Sure, Ferrari will always have the money it requires. But even Williams and McLaren were rocked over the winter when

some of their sponsors failed to renew their contracts. Jordan was hit even harder, with the withdrawal of Deutsche Post. And Minardi also had to go cap in hand, while Arrows finally keeled over. So, budgetary measures such as cutting back on testing will be heeded from here on. And so they should, as Formula One can't afford to lose any more teams.

We've chosen to lighten the tone in our look at the teams' chances in 2003, with an imaginary bar-room conversation on who will shine and who will wilt.

NB As last year, not all of the drivers had been confirmed at the time of going to press, so I've had to take some educated guesses. Indeed, it's possible that some might not have survived. But I expect that they all will have, as Formula One people are fighters.

>> FERRARI

RUNAWAY HORSES

Those Ferrari horses are a-prancing all right. A glance at last year's record of winning 15 of the 17 Grands Prix and scoring as many points as all the other teams put together indicates that the Italian team is right at the top of the pile and it's up to their leading rivals to try and knock them off. With Michael Schumacher and Rubens Barrichello providing the fireworks, expect more magic from the folk from Maranello.

Mr Mastermind: Jean Todt pulled together all the strands to make Ferrari great again.

Win, win, win. What's still to aim for after Michael Schumacher made it three drivers' titles in succession last year, also giving Ferrari its fourth consecutive constructors' crown?

More of the same. After all, Formula One is all about winning, surely? That's what Ferrari's fans expect, and that's what Ferrari no doubt intends to deliver. It's as simple as that.

Talking of the ever excitable tifosi, one question is whether they are cheering for Ferrari, for Michael, or for both?

For both, but the Ferrari name is one that team founder Enzo Ferrari always said counted for more than the drivers. In his day, the drivers were seen as simply being part of the Ferrari equation, to be plugged in, like lightbulbs.

Sure, Enzo wasn't overly romantic. Even the cars were scrapped as soon as they were of no further use. But is it different today as Michael appears to have the team wrapped around his little finger?

No, Monsieur Jean Todt runs the team.

But he appears to be close to Michael?

Yes, they're extremely good friends as well as colleagues. But this isn't surprising as they've gone through a great deal together, as

they turned Ferrari back into a winning team again from 1996 onwards.

Would you say that their relationship is like that between Colin Chapman and Jim Clark in the Lotus glory days?

Precisely.

Do you reckon that it was this friendship that led to the team orders situation in last year's Austrian Grand Prix that caused such a furore when Rubens Barrichello, who had held the upper hand all meeting, was asked to let Michael through to win? Indeed, will Ferrari use such tactics again?

Well, Ferrari said that it was entirely within its rights to do what it did. Besides, Todt said that Michael needed every point possible towards his championship, as Ferrari had missed out on the title before by just a few points at the final round.

Hold on, though, didn't Michael go on to

wrap up last year's title with fully six of the 17 Grands Prix still to run?

Er, yes, but you can never be too careful.

That orchestrated manoeuvre certainly stirred up a hornets' nest, though, with fans still jeering Michael's Ferrari at the following race, at Monaco, and the one after that, in Montreal.

Hold on, this is Formula One, you know, and people who don't understand it allow themselves to get too whipped up by the media.

On a happier note, Rubens won four times last year, ending 2002 as runner-up overall to Michael. How do you think that he'll be feeling this year? Do you think that he'll be motivated to win races, or is he resigned to his fate as Michael's support act?

From the outside, Rubens looks very motivated, as you could see when he really pushed Michael hard in the second half of last year's World Championship. No doubt Ferrari will say that we'll have to wait and see which of its drivers is the more successful.

No guesses as to which of Michael or Rubens will be the faster?

We'll see, but don't forget that it takes a very special driver even to get close to Michael's pace. After all, he is the fastest driver of them all.

With all this talk about Michael and Rubens, it's easy to overlook the sterling job done by the "forgotten men" of Ferrari, test drivers Luca Badoer and Luciano Burti, as they pound around Ferrari's Fiorano and Mugello test tracks week in, week out.

Indeed, they've been a crucial part of Ferrari's success, with Luca concentrating on chassis development and Luciano forging a relationship with Bridgestone that helped develop their tyres throughout the year.

There was much talk last year that "the show" had to be improved, with one suggestion from the sport's governing body, the FIA, being that 1kg of ballast should be added to a driver's car for every point scored. That would have meant that Michael would have been carrying 134kg – the weight of two average-sized adults or one extremely fat one – at Suzuka last October. It's true to say that Ferrari president Luca di Montezemolo was not impressed.

Yes, and rightly so. He said that he found the FIA's proposals "slightly insane" and even suggested that he might take Ferrari out of Formula One to pastures new. After all, isn't Formula One supposed to be about striving to be the best?

Yes, you could have a point there.

Indeed, as it's the very essence of what Formula One is all about.

Even if Ferrari wins every race in 2003?

Yes, even if Ferrari does. But don't expect Williams and McLaren to have sat on their hands and done nothing through the winter. They never do.

Looking at this year's car, the F2003. Ferrari will probably say that it's just a simple step up from the all-beating F2002, but rumour has it that it will have an all-new engine with a shorter stroke and, in turn, a reduction in its length that has enabled the design team to lower the car's centre of gravity.

The rumours might be right. You never know...

That's cagey, but I think we can take it as read that the design team will come up with something special, as will engine guru Paolo Martinelli, Ross Brawn will call the tactical shots from the pit wall and team manager Stefano Domenicali will make the whole show run like clockwork and achieve a finishing record of which other teams can only dream.

On the evidence of 2002, you'd be mad not to reckon that they will.

That's pretty scary for Ferrari's rivals. What do you reckon will be their best course of action?

To go out and buy a Ferrari scarf…

Teamwork Of The Highest Order: Ferrari loves winning Grands Prix, but its success comes through meticulous planning and considerable hard work.

FOR THE RECORD

Country of origin:	**Italy**
Team base:	**Maranello, Italy**
Telephone:	**(39) 0536 949111**
Website:	**www.ferrari.it or www.ferrariworld.it**
Active in Formula One:	**From 1950**
Grands Prix contested:	**670**
Wins:	**159**
Pole positions:	**158**
Fastest laps:	**159**

DRIVERS + RESULTS 2002

Driver	Nationality	Races	Wins	Pts	Pos
Rubens Barrichello	**Brazilian**	**17**	**4**	**77**	**2nd**
Michael Schumacher	**German**	**17**	**11**	**144**	**1st**

THE TEAM

Team principal:	**Jean Todt**
Technical director:	**Ross Brawn**
Team manager:	**Stefano Domenicali**
Chief designer:	**Rory Byrne**
Chief engineer:	**Luca Baldisserri**
Test drivers:	**Luca Badoer & Luciano Burti**
Chassis:	**Ferrari F2003**
Engine:	**Ferrari V10**
Tyres:	**Bridgestone**

MICHAEL SCHUMACHER

POETRY IN MOTION

Michael made winning look easy last year when he broke yet more records as he pulled level with Juan Manuel Fangio on five world titles. This year, the great German is tipped to make it six.

TRACK NOTES

Nationality	GERMAN
Born	3 JANUARY, 1969, KERPEN, GERMANY
Website	www.michael-schumacher.de
Teams	JORDAN 1991, BENETTON 1991–1995, FERRARI 1996–2003

Flying finale: Michael sprays the bubbly at Suzuka after rounding out 2002 with his 11th triumph of a record-breaking season.

If anyone thinks that Michael might start to back off, think again, as he loves racing, and loves winning even more. Why stop at 64 wins when you can aim at 100?

After winning titles three and four in 2000 and 2001, it was always likely that Michael would make it five. But what no-one had envisaged was how superb the Ferrari 2002 would be and how well its tailor-made Bridgestone tyres would work. We expected Michael to use his talents to the full, but, in truth, he didn't even have to. Indeed, had team orders late in the year not urged him to support team-mate Barrichello, his record tally of 11 wins would've been higher still.

Starting last year with his 2001 car, Michael won in Melbourne. A clash with Montoya at Sepang was a blow – his third-place was a season's worst finish – before the arrival of the F2002 in Brazil made it plain that Ferrari had moved up a gear. He won, added two more and then claimed a fourth at the A1-Ring. But that race in Austria rocked Michael as he was exposed to the wrath of the crowd after Barrichello was told to let him through. When Michael nipped past Raikkonen to win at Magny-Cours, the title was his, with six races to go. Michael's best drive came at Spa, then he could have won at Indianapolis but messed up a photo finish, before scoring win number 11 at Suzuka.

CAREER RECORD

First Grand Prix	1991 BELGIAN GP
Grand Prix starts	179
Grand Prix wins	64

(1992 Belgian GP, 1993 Portuguese GP, 1994 Brazilian GP, Pacific GP, San Marino GP, Monaco GP, Canadian GP, French GP, Hungarian GP, European GP, 1995 Brazilian GP, Spanish GP, Monaco GP, French GP, German GP, Belgian GP, European GP, Pacific GP, Japanese GP, 1996 Spanish GP, Belgian GP, Italian GP, 1997 Monaco GP, Canadian GP, French GP, Belgian GP, Japanese GP, 1998 Argentinian GP, Canadian GP, French GP, British GP, Hungarian GP, Italian GP, 1999 San Marino GP, Monaco GP, 2000 Australian GP, Brazilian GP, San Marino GP, European GP, Canadian GP, Italian GP, US GP, Japanese GP, Malaysian GP, 2001 Australian GP, Malaysian GP, Spanish GP, Monaco GP, European GP, French GP, Hungarian GP, Belgian GP, Japanese GP, 2002 Australian GP, Brazilian GP, San Marino GP, Spanish GP, Austrian GP, Canadian GP, British GP, French GP, German GP, Belgian GP, Japanese GP)

Poles	50
Fastest laps	50
Points	945

Honours   2002, 2001, 2000, 1995 & 1994 FORMULA ONE CHAMPION, 1998 FORMULA ONE RUNNER-UP, 1990 GERMAN FORMULA THREE CHAMPION & MACAU GP WINNER, 1988 GERMAN FORMULA KONIG CHAMPION

Win, win, win

A childhood in karts left Michael set fair for a career in cars, but his skills exceeded expectations and he was such a star in Formula Three that Mercedes snapped him up to race sportscars. Michael was given his Formula One break in 1991 when Bertrand Gachot was jailed, leaving a vacancy at Jordan. So impressive was his speed that Benetton put him straight onto its payroll. He rewarded them with world titles in 1994 and 1995. But the challenge of helping Ferrari rediscover its former glory was too much for Michael to resist and he moved there in 1996, winning three races and an increasing number thereafter. Indeed, had he not been pipped by Mika Hakkinen in 1998 then broken a leg in 1999, he could already have that sixth or even seventh world title.

RUBENS BARRICHELLO

A MOUNTAIN TO CLIMB

Rubens finished last year as runner-up in the drivers' championship, but despite his improvement in form, don't expect him to force Ferrari team-mate Michael Schumacher off the top of the perch.

Rubens must be dreaming that he can continue the progression that has seen him rank fourth overall in 2000, third in 2001 and runner-up in 2002. However, he knows that to do so he must overcome his Ferrari team-mate Michael Schumacher.

Rubens made it clear last May why he'd re-signed for two more years, saying "Ferrari keeps me in the team because they love me racing the car." Trouble was, just two days later, as he was heading for victory in Austria, Ferrari showed that they loved Michael that little bit more and told Rubens to let him through. Ferrari spent much of the rest of last year trying to make things up to Rubens.

Rubens will have to improve on last year's four wins if he's ever to do anything other than wait around at Ferrari until Michael retires and lets him take over as number one. However, if that doesn't happen at the end of 2004, it may never happen.

Qualifying on pole for the first of last year's races, in Melbourne, promised great things, but Rubens was taken out by Ralf Schumacher on the run to the first corner. Hopes of winning in Brazil were thwarted when he passed Michael for the lead, then almost immediately pulled off. Second at Imola wasn't matched until that controversial day at the A1-Ring.

But it all came right at the Nurburgring when he led from start to finish thanks to a light fuel load moving him from fourth to first on the opening lap. This wasn't matched until Michael had clinched his third title for Ferrari, with win number two coming at the Hungaroring. Then, his two-stop strategy proved just faster than Michael's one-stopper at Monza for number three. Michael messing up a photo finish at Indianapolis gave Rubens number four.

Nationality	**BRAZILIAN**
Born	23 MAY, 1972, SAO PAULO, BRAZIL
Website	www.barrichello.com.br
Teams	JORDAN 1993–1996, STEWART 1997–1999, FERRARI 2000–2003

CAREER RECORD

First Grand Prix	1993 SOUTH AFRICAN GP
Grand Prix starts	164
Grand Prix wins	5 (2000 German GP, 2002 European GP, Hungarian GP, Italian GP, US GP)
Poles	6
Fastest laps	8
Points	272
Honours	2002 FORMULA ONE RUNNER-UP, 1991 BRITISH FORMULA THREE CHAMPION, 1990 EUROPEAN FORMULA OPEL CHAMPION, 1988 BRAZILIAN KART CHAMPION

A surprised winner: Rubens didn't know he'd won at Indianapolis until he reached the podium.

Helped all the way

When Rubens decided to race in Europe his sponsors clubbed together and, for a cut, backed him all the way to Formula One. Making the most of their support, he won the Formula Opel Euroseries in 1990, beat David Coulthard to the British Formula Three title in 1991, then finished third overall in Formula 3000 in 1992. Jordan snapped him up and Rubens stunned the Formula One world by running second to Ayrton Senna at Donington Park in his third outing. His car broke, but the world took heed. Second in the 1995 Canadian GP was his best result in his next three years with Jordan, and it wasn't until a shock second at Monaco in 1997 with Stewart that he peaked again. Then, in 2000, Rubens went to Ferrari, claiming the win that his talent deserved in the wet 2000 German GP.

>> WILLIAMS

AIMING HIGH AGAIN

Williams and BMW will have worked like mad over the winter in their quest to build the pace-setting hardware to take the battle to Ferrari after having their noses comprehensively bloodied last year.

Do you think that Ferrari can be beaten in 2003?

Of course they can, but the goalposts are always moving, as Ferrari proved last year.

Williams have stated that the only way to take on Ferrari would be with a radical new car. Do you think that this is within their capabilities?

Well, Formula One fans certainly hope so. To be honest, you only need to glance at their track record to know that it is.

What's so different about this year's car?

Why not take a look for yourself and see whether you can spot the changes.

Er, is the nose a little higher, the tail a little lower and the sides a little more scalloped? Is the blue of the livery a little darker?

Good grief... I suppose, that's why you're a journalist and they run a racing team.

The team's engine supplier, BMW, was the first to break the 19,000rpm barrier last year. What are the chances that they will top 20,000rpm in 2003?

If that's what it takes, that's what they'll do to stay ahead of the game. BMW aren't in this to come second. In fact, they're making noises about being champions in 2004.

Revs are one thing, but horsepower is the crux. Will BMW be the first engine manufacturer to top 900bhp?

We'll only find out if the likes of Ferrari and McLaren are left choking on their dust.

If BMW really aims for the sky, is 1000bhp possible?

It might be. After all, it's a nice round figure, something of a landmark, although the turbo engines used in the late 1980s, with BMW leading the way, produced up to 1300bhp in qualifying. And then melted...

Is it all rosy in the BMW camp, with engine project leader Werner Franz jumping ship to join arch-rivals Mercedes, and one of his underlings in the engine department, Heinz Paschen, replacing him. Do you reckon that this will hamper progress?

Not in 2003 as Werner won't start at Mercedes until April, so his impact won't be felt until 2004. However, no engine department is the work of one person, so BMW won't be destroyed by his departure, especially as Heinz has been part of the BMW programme for three years and has quite a pedigree.

Looking back to 2002, Juan Pablo Montoya was on pole for race after race mid-season. Five in all, actually, so why didn't he win any of those races?

Eagle Eye: Nothing gets past Sir Frank Williams as he and partner Patrick Head fight to get their illustrious team back to the front.

THE VIPS

SAM MICHAEL

Much like Ferrari and McLaren, every Formula One fan knows that Williams is headed by Sir Frank Williams and Patrick Head, but Sam has become one of the men who matter ever since, at the German's request, he followed Ralf Schumacher across from Jordan. A clear head in a frantic world, this 31-year-old Australian race engineer started in Formula One with Lotus in 1994 before working at Jordan from 1995 to 2000.

MARIO THEISSEN

Not so long ago, the man in charge of engines wouldn't have been considered as being as important as those designing the cars. But this has all changed, especially in the case of BMW, with Dr Theissen's employers providing the pick of the engines in the Formula One paddock. With BMW since graduating in 1977, Mario teamed up with Gerhard Berger on the motorsport programme in 1999, with responsibility for all the programme's technical functions.

There was a problem with the car eating its tyres in race trim. And then there was Michael, his Ferrari and those Bridgestone tyres...

There was a feeling midway through 2002 that Williams's other driver Ralf Schumacher wasn't quite matching Juan Pablo for speed. Does this hold true?

No, that's mainly a perception. In fact, Ralf tended to be every bit as fast as Juan Pablo in the races, but not always in qualifying.

You might have a point, but a glance at the records shows that Juan Pablo outqualified Ralf only 9–8, so it was closer than most people recall.

That does surprise me. Mind you, that shows what a balanced pair of drivers they are.

There was none of the end-of-the-year drop-off last year that we've seen from Ralf in previous seasons when first Jenson

FOR THE RECORD

Country of origin:	England
Team base:	Grove, England
Telephone:	(44) 01235 777700
Website:	www.bmw.williamsf1.com or
	www.williamsf1.co.uk
Active in Formula One:	From 1973
Grands Prix contested:	462
Wins:	108
Pole positions:	119
Fastest laps:	122

DRIVERS + RESULTS 2002

Driver	Nationality	Races	Wins	Pts	Pos
Juan Pablo Montoya	Colombian	17	1	50	3rd
Ralf Schumacher	German	17	1	42	4th

THE TEAM

Team principal:	Sir Frank Williams
Technical director:	Patrick Head
Team manager:	Dickie Stanford
Chief designer:	Gavin Fisher
Chief engineer:	Sam Michael
Test driver:	Marc Gene
Chassis:	Williams FW25
Engine:	BMW V10
Tyres:	Michelin

Looking ahead: Patrick Head studies the form and plots a future in which Williams challenges for World Championship glory once more.

head-up display. Do you reckon this is a little "fancy pants", or will it give him an advantage?

I reckon that he's got the right idea, as it will supply data – such as dangers on the track ahead or dropping oil pressure – to the periphery of his vision, rather than the team having to relay it to him via a display on his steering wheel. This will let him see the data without having to stop focusing on the track ahead. So, yes, it's sensible rather than "fancy pants".

It would be quite an advantage if he's neck-and-neck with Juan Pablo heading for the first corner then?

Ho ho. But, yes, actually.

Looking at the hardware involved in running a team, a state-of-the-art wind tunnel remains the thing to have. So, the news that Williams is building a second tunnel has to be positive. After all, Ferrari has three.

Actually, the second tunnel won't be ready until 2004, but Williams has already employed extra aerodynamicists, John Davis from Minardi and Antonia Terzi from Ferrari.

This ought to placate BMW, as they suggested in 2002 that Williams might want to improve its chassis to match their engines?

I can see where you're coming from.

What of rumours that 50 BMW engineers would be moving to Williams' base to help with the design and build of the FW25, to make it more integrated, like the Ferrari?

Until proved otherwise, they're just that, rumours, although BMW's Mario Theissen said last October that BMW had the option of either building its own chassis, continuing with Williams in a "more appropriate form", or even quitting Formula One.

Blimey! Mind you, Williams' deal with BMW runs out at the end of 2003, so there could be a danger that BMW will "do a Ferrari" and build their own chassis to go with their engine.

That's unlikely as BMW would have had to have started building a chassis midway through 2002 so that they could spend 2003 testing, just as Toyota did in 2001 for their 2002 race debut.

Judging by the (lack of) success of Toyota's bid last year, perhaps BMW might want to consider two years of testing first?

Well, it's not as easy as it looks to build a winning chassis. It certainly doesn't happen overnight.

Button then Juan Pablo assumed the upper hand.

Yes, Ralf got it back together and was a real match for Juan Pablo as summer turned to autumn.

It could be said that they were too much of a match, as they tripped each other up on the first lap at Monza and on the second lap at Indianapolis. It's an understatement to say that this failed to impress the team.

Yup, I don't think they'll want reminding. However, unlike Ferrari, Williams likes its drivers to race, but it also likes them to engage their brains.

In view of tales that Ralf and Juan Pablo aren't exactly the best of buddies, would you say that they make ideal dinner companions for each other?

They're very different people, but they do have one thing in common: they both drive for Williams. And at least they seemed to acknowledge each other in 2002.

Ralf will be using a special helmet with a "fighter pilot" style

JUAN PABLO MONTOYA

THE HEIR APPARENT

Spurred on by a disappointing second year with Williams, when Ferrari reigned supreme, Juan Pablo Montoya will be champing at the bit to get some more wins under his belt in 2003.

Montoya craves success. For him, the thrill of gathering pole positions by the handful, as in 2002, won't satisfy him again. He wants wins. He wants to be tilting at the title, especially if that means going head-to-head with Michael Schumacher. For that, he's going to need a car/engine combination that can match the best Ferrari and, perhaps, McLaren can offer. And tyres from Michelin that are as good to race on as the best from Bridgestone.

This chirpy Colombian is loved at Williams, with Frank Williams and Patrick Head fond of his ever-attacking style, and the mechanics adoring his jokey attitude. He acts as though he's one of them. For the press, he can be moody, but he's good for a quote.

In case things don't go his way, Juan Pablo has positioned himself well by signing a contract that keeps him with Williams until the end of 2004, crucially leaving him free when Schumacher is expected to quit Ferrari. Rest assured, if he gets hands on a winning car, he'll win races.

Having been on the pace at the end of 2001, Juan Pablo expected to start winning from the outset of last season. But, after dicing with Michael Schumacher at Melbourne, he had to settle for second. He was second again at Sepang after clashing with Michael at the first corner.

Taking his car's nose off against Michael's Ferrari at Interlagos cost him a good result, but from then on, despite qualifying on pole for five consecutive races, Juan Pablo was seldom able to match the red cars. Certainly, he ran second at Monaco until his engine blew, suffered a similar fate at Montreal and finished second at Hockenheim, but he spent much of the year thinking "roll on 2003", with only a pair of clashes with his team-mate Ralf Schumacher marking out the late-season races.

TRACK NOTES

Nationality	COLOMBIAN
Born	20 SEPTEMBER, 1975, BOGOTA, COLOMBIA
Website	www.jpmontoya.com
Teams	WILLIAMS 2001–2003

CAREER RECORD

First Grand Prix	2001 AUSTRALIAN GP
Grand Prix starts	34
Grand Prix wins	1 (2001 Italian GP)
Poles	10
Fastest laps	6
Points	81
Honours	2000 INDY 500 WINNER, 1999 INDYCAR CHAMPION, 1998 FORMULA 3000 CHAMPION

Groomed by Williams

After showing speed in the American Barber Dodge Pro-Series in 1994, in British Formula Vauxhall in 1995 and British Formula Three the following year, it was when Juan Pablo reached Formula 3000 that he came into his own, albeit having too many accidents. He got his act together in 1998, though, beating Nick Heidfeld to the crown. A test driver for Williams that year, there was no race seat for him in 1999, so Juan Pablo was seconded to the USA and won the ChampCar title, following this by winning the Indy 500 in 2000. He announced his arrival in Formula One at Williams with a bang in 2001, with his maiden win coming in the Italian GP as he established himself as the faster of the two Williams drivers.

Can grinners be winners?: Juan Pablo enjoyed qualifying on pole position on numerous occasions in 2002, but he would assuredly have traded any of these for a race win.

RALF SCHUMACHER

FINGERS CROSSED

TRACK NOTES

Ralf Schumacher, like team-mate Juan-Pablo Montoya, will be praying that Williams, BMW and Michelin can offer him a competitive package with which to take the battle to the Ferraris, especially to his brother Michael.

Nationality	GERMAN
Born	30 JUNE, 1975, KERPEN, GERMANY
Website	www.ralf-schumacher.de
Teams	JORDAN 1997–1998, WILLIAMS 1999–2003

CAREER RECORD

First Grand Prix	1997
	AUSTRALIAN GP
Grand Prix starts	100
Grand Prix wins	4
(2001 San Marino GP, Canadian GP, German GP, 2002 Malaysian GP)	
Poles	1
Fastest laps	6
Points	177
Honours	1996 FORMULA NIPPON CHAMPION, 1995 GERMAN FORMULA THREE RUNNER-UP & MACAU GP WINNER, 1993 GERMAN FORMEL JUNIOR RUNNER-UP

All Smiles: Ralf lightened up a little in 2002, but he will only have a permanent smile if he starts winning more frequently this year, as his tally of one win in 2002 left him disappointed.

It's strange to report that last year, as much as his first in Formula One in 1997, established Ralf's credentials to be seen as one of the top drivers. Certainly, four years had passed, including the 2001 season that contained his first three wins, but it was his consistent speed in 2002 that marked a new-found maturity.

Indeed, all talk that Ralf had gone off the boil in the second half of the previous few seasons, when partnered by Jenson Button and then Juan Pablo Montoya, was put to rest as he was "on it" right to the end. If anything, Ralf became even more effective as the season progressed, with his application seeming better and his relationship with Williams personnel stronger than before. The only area in which he suffered in comparison was qualifying.

The start to his season was spectacular when a clash with Barrichello on the run to the first corner at Melbourne sent him skywards. Using his repaired chassis, he won next time out at Sepang, albeit thanks to his brother Michael and Montoya clashing at the first corner. A second behind Michael at Interlagos kept his momentum going, but he was never to match these two results in the remaining 14 races as Ferrari stamped their mark. Third places at Imola, Monaco, Hockenheim and Hungaroring helped keep Montoya in check, but incidents with his team-mate on the opening lap at Monza and on the second lap at Indianapolis were not what the doctor ordered. And certainly not Patrick Head...

His own man

Being the son a famous father is one thing, but being the brother of a famous driver is even harder, as you're compared on a level playing field, rather than one skewed by changes of equipment over time. So it was that all eyes turned to Ralf as he graduated from karts. When he didn't make an instant impact and seemed arrogant, his name was sullied. However, Ralf came good in Formula Three in 1994 and won the Macau GP in 1995. Racing in Formula Nippon – Japan's Formula 3000 – in 1996, Ralf won the title. This helped him reach Formula One in 1997 with Jordan. He was third on his third outing, albeit after knocking team-mate Giancarlo Fisichella off. Angry at not being allowed to challenge team-mate Damon Hill for victory at the Belgian GP in 1998, Ralf joined Williams in 1999, scoring consistently as BMW's engine advanced. Had he not suffered a puncture at the Nurburgring, he'd have won there. Sixth overall that year, he advanced to fifth in 2000 and fourth in 2001.

>> McLAREN

BRONZE IS NOT ENOUGH

West McLaren-Mercedes slipped to third overall last year and Ron Dennis didn't like it. Bear in mind that he's the one who once said that he woke up in pain on Monday mornings if his team hadn't won the previous day's grand prix.

THE VIPS

STEVE HALLAM
Think McLaren and it's Ron Dennis and design chief Adrian Newey who spring to mind. Well, it's time that more people were made aware of Steve's input. Engineer to Ayrton Senna at Lotus, Steve joined McLaren in 1991, guiding Mika Hakkinen to the 1998 and 1999 world titles. He's now in charge of race engineering.

MARIO ILIEN
Half of the partnership with the late Paul Morgan that made Ilmor one of the world's greatest racing engine builders, this Swiss engineer has a CV that includes a spell at Cosworth from 1979. It was here that he met Morgan and formed Ilmor in 1984, building winning Indycar engines until Mercedes wanted a Formula One engine. With Mercedes buying an ever larger share in Ilmor, the finance will soon be in place for ever greater feats.

The Boss: Ron Dennis is more than a figurehead at McLaren, as he *is* McLaren, taking a hands-on role at every Grand Prix.

Acknowledging that last season wasn't one that McLaren will recall with any pleasure, what do you reckon would have been the most galling sight for them in 2002?

Watching Bridgestone's tyre supremo Hirohide Hamashima sit alongside the Ferrari big-wigs on the Ferrari pitwall as their tyres lorded it over the Michelins with a success rate of 15:2 over those on Michelins.

Yes, that must have been particularly painful, as, until the end of 2001, McLaren was on Bridgestones too.

A great proportion of Ferrari's advantage last year came from having a tyre developed specifically for their use, whereas Michelin had to divide its attack between McLaren and Williams.

Mentioning that, there was talk last year that McLaren and Williams would pool their tyre development findings in order to fight back against the cars in red.

Rest assured, these teams will do anything it takes to beat Ferrari and get back to the front.

At the start of 2002, Ron Dennis predicted that Ferrari would win fewer races than in 2001 when they won nine of the 17 Grands Prix. In fact, it went the other way and they won 15. Why do you think that he was so wrong in his prediction?

The tyre situation: no one could have predicted that Bridgestone would have become so dominant.

All right, let's stop mentioning those round, black things.

That's probably for the best.

David Coulthard isn't known for his love of a car that doesn't handle to his liking. How much did he like the MP4-17?

You might have noticed that he won at Monaco with it, so it can't have been all bad.

I don't suppose his team-mate Kimi Raikkonen has won the hearts of the team with his witty repartee?

Well, you'd be surprised... Actually, it's not one of his strong points. But he is very, very fast.

Another one who didn't appear to be smiling much in 2002 was technical director Adrian Newey. Does he ever smile?

Oh yes, but not often when he's at the track. Especially not last year. He's an extremely focused individual, you know.

McLaren is renowned for its love of continuity, is this why they've stuck with David and Kimi for 2003?

Yes and no, as while continuity makes sense and provides the team with stability, McLaren have also stuck with them as they think they can do the job, providing that they're equipped with competitive machinery.

Talking of which, what steps will have had to be made to close the gap to Ferrari?

Adrian and the design team will have had to design a car that pushes the boundaries of performance, just as Ferrari did last year.

There's new blood in the design team, too, as Mike Coughlan was snapped up from Arrows midway through last year.

If he's as good as his reputation, he'll be a strong addition to Newey's crew.

I hear that there's no new McLaren for the first few races of 2003, just an update of the MP4-17 known as the MP4-17D. Is this wise since the MP4-17 won just once in 2002?

Insiders say that McLaren know there's more to come from what they've got, as shown in 2002 by Ferrari, who won the first two races before introducing the F2002 at the Brazilian GP. This approach should at least have a greater potential for reliability in those first three races before the Formula One teams

FOR THE RECORD

Country of origin:	England
Team base:	Woking, England
Telephone:	(44) 01483 728211
Website:	www.mclaren.com
Active in Formula One:	From 1966
Grands Prix contested:	543
Wins:	135
Pole positions:	112
Fastest laps:	109

DRIVERS + RESULTS 2002

Driver	Nationality	Races	Wins	Pts	Pos
David Coulthard	Scottish	17	1	41	5th
Kimi Raikkonen	Finnish	17	-	24	6th

THE TEAM

Team principal:	Ron Dennis
Technical director:	Adrian Newey
Team manager:	David Ryan
Chief designer:	Neil Oatley
Chief engineer:	Steve Hallam
Third driver:	Alexander Wurz
Chassis:	McLaren MP4-18
Engine:	Mercedes V10
Tyres:	Michelin

return to Europe for the San Marino GP.

Although Adrian Newey reckons that starting the season with the revised car may produce points through reliability, surely such a tactic won't help McLaren win the championship in 2003?

The team will be hoping that Adrian is wrong. On the second charge, that is...

Mercedes is taking more of a stake in Ilmor, what chance this will lead to greater horsepower?

Well, the all-new engine will be smaller and lighter than last year's lump, so... With Mercedes upping its share of Ilmor from 25 per cent to 55 per cent, you can be sure that they'll be trying to have more of an influence over design and development, which can't be a bad thing. By the way, the company will henceforth be called Mercedes-Ilmor.

New name, new ambition, it seems, as they've shown their intent by enticing BMW engine chief Werner Franz to head their project. Do you think he's the missing piece in the puzzle?

He just may be, especially if his arrival lets Mario Ilien do what he does best, design engines.

Talking Shop: David Coulthard and technical director Adrian Newey work hard to try and close the gap on Ferrari, and will be hoping for more than the one win they managed in 2002 in the campaign ahead.

I hear that Werner won't have any influence on this year's Mercedes-Ilmor engine.

Well, Werner isn't free to start work until the end of April, so it's safe to say that his focus will be on the 2004 motor.

Might all this mean that Mercedes-Ilmor ups sticks from Northamptonshire and bases itself in Stuttgart when Mercedes acquires 100 per cent ownership in 2005?

No, but Mercedes will use some of its facilities in Stuttgart to help the project.

It seemed for a while that McLaren might have spent the winter with the conundrum of having three drivers to fit into two race seats, as Mika Hakkinen also had a contract for 2003. Was it ever possible that he'd decide to return to racing, or did the team know that he'd turn his sabbatical into retirement?

Actually, they didn't know for sure, until he came to Monaco to face the press.

Retirement or not, will Mika be seen at any races this year, or do you think he'll be enjoying himself too much among the trees and lakes of his native Finland?

He's a man who enjoys peace and quiet...

McLaren does have a third driver, though, in Alexander Wurz. His role, as well as being the reserve in case of injury to David or Kimi, is presumably to continue leading the team's test and development programme?

Yes, and he's excellent at this, with a bright and technical mind, as well as the ability to lap right on the pace too.

Always looking for an edge, McLaren's impressive Team Communications Centre was a hit in the paddock last year as it towered over the other teams' motorhomes. Ron Dennis even said that it helped the symbiosis of the team. What chance that this ground-breaker will be followed in 2003 by revolutionary cool suits to be worn by the pit crew?

That's a possibility, as they've developed a liquid-fed suit and helmet to help keep the crew cool in the extreme heat and humidity of places such as Sepang.

In short, will McLaren and Mercedes bounce back from a season that both described as "disappointing"?

Miracles don't happen overnight, but rest assured that they're working on it. Working very, very hard.

DAVID COULTHARD

A NEED TO WIN

A poor package left David Coulthard frustrated through 2002, but the pace of his team-mate Kimi Raikkonen will also have worried him. So, this is a very important year for the accomplished Scot.

Back for an eighth year with McLaren, David knows that he must deliver this year as, whatever the level of competitiveness of the McLaren-Mercedes combination, he is up against a team-mate in Raikkonen who started to show him a clean pair of heels in qualifying last year.

Certainly, the McLaren-Mercedes package was no dream in 2002, the car struggling for balance, the fact that its Michelins were generally no match for Ferrari's Bridgestone rubber come the race, and the fact that its engine was not leading the horsepower stakes. For this year's campaign, though, expect Mercedes to have got their sums right. Expect, too, that Michelin will be more clued up, especially if McLaren and Williams pool tyre data. Thirdly, expect McLaren to produce a more effective chassis, with Adrian Newey having his eye more on the ball than during 2001 when he was being enticed by Jaguar.

Grabbing the lead of last season's first race after Rubens Barrichello and Ralf Schumacher collided was a great start, but a gearbox glitch put David out. After another failure at Sepang, David started a run of six point-scoring races, with his blast past pole-sitter Juan Pablo Montoya at Monaco leading to a famous win under pressure from Michael Schumacher. A wild move into the chicane took him into second ahead of Barrichello at Montreal next time out, with his Michelins working well David was third at Magny-Cours, then late-season car improvements helped him to third at Indianapolis. He was set for the same at Suzuka before car trouble.

Dreaming Of Victory: David looks thoughtful as he contemplates his and McLaren's chances in the forthcoming 16 Grands Prix.

TRACK NOTES

Nationality	**SCOTTISH**
Born	**27 MARCH, 1971,**
	TWYNHOLM, SCOTLAND
Website	www.davidcoulthard.co.uk
Teams	**WILLIAMS 1994–1995,**
	McLAREN 1996–2003

CAREER RECORD

First Grand Prix	**1994 SPANISH GP**
Grand Prix starts	**141**
Grand Prix wins	**12**
	(1995 Portuguese GP, 1997
	Australian GP, Italian GP, 1998 San
	Marino GP, 1999 British GP, Belgian
	GP, 2000 British GP, Monaco GP,
	French GP, 2001 Brazilian GP,
	Austrian GP, 2002 Monaco GP)
Poles	**12**
Fastest laps	**18**
Points	**400**
Honours	**2001 FORMULA ONE**
	RUNNER-UP, 1991 BRITISH FORMULA
	THREE RUNNER-UP & MACAU GP
	WINNER, 1989 McLAREN
	AUTOSPORT YOUNG DRIVER OF THE
	YEAR & BRITISH JUNIOR FORMULA
	FORD CHAMPION, 1988 SCOTTISH
	KART CHAMPION

The Flying Scot

David could do no wrong as he rocketed through karts and the junior single-seater categories. And the most important thing he won was the McLaren Autosport Young Driver scholarship at the end of 1989, his first year in cars, for this gave him a test run in a McLaren. His speed and poise impressed and a relationship started that runs strong today. While this eased his passage to Formula One, it didn't guarantee it and David nearly faltered when he was faced with finding the budget for a third year of Formula 3000. However, he was saved by being test driver for Williams and being asked to step up when Ayrton Senna died in 1994. He rounded out that season with second place in the Portuguese GP, the race that yielded his first GP win in 1995. His management team took David to McLaren, a move that has done him well since, but took him from Williams just as it hit its richest form. In the subsequent years, all partnering Mika Hakkinen until last year, he added at least one win every year, but he was outpaced by Mika as he claimed the 1998 and 1999 titles.

KIMI RAIKKONEN

READY TO WIN

Kimi Raikkonen did everything that his supporters expected of him last year, and more, but he'll be hoping for a more competitive car in his second season with McLaren so that he can take that elusive first win.

Kimi is the new ice man. In fact, he's more than taken over the title from compatriot Mika Hakkinen, he's taken it to a new level. Try making him flustered and you'll see. There won't be a flicker. Try to make him laugh or show any emotion and it'll be a struggle. He's here in Formula One to win races, even titles. Nothing else matters.

His speed is shown by his 10:7 advantage over team-mate David Coulthard in qualifying last year. He also has developed the race craft to go for victory. However, Ferrari's clear advantage meant that it was very difficult for a driver from any other team to claim the top step of the podium. Kimi came extraordinarily close to being one of the few to do so in the French GP when he was leading with five laps to go and slipped on oil, letting Michael Schumacher through to win.

Kimi's second year in Formula One – but first with McLaren – started with third at Melbourne, but it could so easily have been second as he outbraked himself on emerging from the pits just ahead of Montoya. What marked the races that followed was speed that was close to Coulthard's, but a string of retirements. This was finally broken at the Canadian GP when he finished fourth after being slowed by a malfunctioning fuel rig. He stepped up a gear at the Nurburgring to be third behind the Ferraris after Coulthard and Montoya clashed. After the disappointment of Magny-Cours, Kimi continued to outqualify Coulthard but was no match when it came to getting his car to the finish, although he benefitted when the Scot's car failed at Suzuka and he came third.

TRACK NOTES

Nationality	FINNISH
Born	17 OCTOBER, 1979, ESPOO, FINLAND
Website	www.kimiraikkonen.com
Teams	SAUBER 2001, McLAREN 2002–2003

CAREER RECORD

First Grand Prix	2001 AUSTRALIAN GP
Grand Prix starts	34
Grand Prix wins	0
	(best result: second 2002 French GP)
Poles	0
Fastest laps	1
Points	33
Honours	2000 BRITISH FORMULA RENAULT CHAMPION, 1999 BRITISH FORMULA RENAULT WINTER SERIES CHAMPION, 1998 EUROPEAN SUPER A KART RUNNER-UP & FINNISH KART CHAMPION & NORDIC KART CHAMPION

On The Podium: Kimi got within a few laps of his first victory in 2002. Expect better this year.

Kimi's big break

Being spotted in the European Karting Championships in 1998 was Kimi's big break. The person who found him was ex-racer Steve Robertson whose father David was managing Jenson Button. After being withdrawn from Formula Renault in 1999 as his team wasn't competitive, Kimi was back in 2000 and won the British title. Only the audacious would have looked to jump straight to Formula 3000. But even that wasn't enough for the Robertsons who urged Sauber to give him a test. They were bowled over by Kimi's immediate speed and cool attitude. And so he was signed for 2001, with just 23 car races to his name. Amazingly, he scored a point on his debut, chased the Ferraris at Imola until his steering wheel came off and peaked with a pair of fourths, which were enough to convince McLaren that he was their future.

>> RENAULT

WAITING TO BE NOTICED

Renault ranked fourth overall last year almost without anyone noticing. But then it's only the top-three teams that caught the eye, which is something the French manufacturer will want to change.

Is Renault still pretending that 2002 was Renault's first year back in Formula One?

They have no reason to pretend this, as that's the truth.

If you insist. So, you think that Renault is happy to continue to ignore the 2001 season when it supplied works engines and some mechanical assistance to Benetton?

That was Benetton, not Renault. Heh, heh!

There was quite a fuss in Britain last July when Renault announced that it was dropping Jenson Button for 2003 and signing 2001 Minardi racer Fernando Alonso – a driver without a point to his name – in his place. Especially as Flavio Briatore happens to be Fernando's manager.

Yes he is. Just how good Fernando is, is hard to say, but Flavio is sure that, in time, he'll be very special.

It had looked at one point as if Fernando might go to Jaguar instead. Was there any possibility of this happening?

Well, he went testing with them and if you asked former boss Niki Lauda, he would have told you how good Fernando is.

So, that means that Flavio must be pleased that he snapped up Fernando so early in his career?

Like all good businessmen, he likes to buy low and sell higher...

Surely there must have been some pressure from Renault for the team to take a French driver?

No, not at all, as Renault prides itself on being an international corporation.

How about pressure to take on an up-

and-coming French driver for the team's test and development programme?*

Well, Formula 3000 champion Sebastien Bourdais is pretty well qualified for this, don't you think?

Jarno Trulli – another of the drivers managed by Flavio – is staying on for a second year with Renault. Presumably the team doesn't share the opinion of many paddock critics that he's excellent over one lap but not so good in a race. Not as good as Jenson, for example, who outscored him 14–9 last year.

There's nothing wrong with Jarno's racing. He just suffers from bad luck, especially if you

THE VIPS

FLAVIO BRIATORE

The day-to-day running of the Renault team is beneath this flamboyant Italian. But don't underestimate the influence that he has, especially with the stable of top-level drivers he has under contract. These don't only include his 2003 charges Fernando Alonso and Jarno Trulli, but also Giancarlo Fisichella and Mark Webber. Yes, one fifth of the Formula One grid. Flavio still insists that he has no interest in Formula One, but it's clearly more than money that keeps him involved.

MIKE GASCOYNE

Known as "The Bulldog", Mike is the brains of Renault's operation, the one whose first major task after joining from Jordan was to restructure the way the design team worked. His racing experience began with McLaren in 1989 where he was an aerodynamicist. A move in 1991 took Mike to Tyrrell, where he stayed until 1997, with a brief break at Sauber. Jordan was his next home before joining Benetton which, of course, metamorphosed into Renault.

At the Helm: Mike Gascoyne is the man who leads Renault's quest for technical excellence in the team's bid to start challenging Formula One's top three of Ferrari, Williams and McLaren.

FOR THE RECORD

Country of origin:	England
Team base:	Enstone, England
Telephone:	(44) 01608 678000
Website:	www.renaultf1.com
Active in Formula One:	From 1986 (as Benetton)
Grands Prix contested:	378
Wins:	27
Pole positions:	16
Fastest laps:	35

DRIVERS + RESULTS 2002

Driver	Nationality	Races	Wins	Pts	Pos
Jenson Button	English	17	-	14	7th
Jarno Trulli	Italian	17	-	9	8th

THE TEAM

Team principal:	Flavio Briatore
Technical director:	Mike Gascoyne
Team manager:	Steve Nielsen
Chief designer:	Tim Densham
Chief engineer:	Pat Symonds
Test driver:	Allan McNish
Chassis:	Renault R203
Engine:	Renault V10
Tyres:	Michelin

Perma Tanned: Flavio Briatore brings a little sunshine to the paddock and is far more determined that his playboy image would suggest.

look at the number of potential point-scoring drives that ended in retirement.

Fair enough. On another tack, it was reckoned that last year's Renault engine had the least power of any in Formula One, bar the Asiatech, pushing out 50bhp less than BMW's monster. I take it that there will be more power on tap this year?

Certainly. Or Flavio and Jean-Jacques His will be most unhappy.

Jarno stated late last year that it wasn't just the engine's power that needed to be sorted, but its reliability too.

I'm sure that he did. He's very perceptive, you know. That's why Flavio thinks he's got the makings of a world champion: he knows what he wants.

Renault is apparently sticking with the wide-vee engine that it pioneered in 2001, whereas everyone else has engines closer to 90 degrees. Who do you think is right?

Well, Renault has every confidence in their engine and engineers.

Ah yes, but rumour has it that Renault would have gone the 90 degree route for 2003 had it thought about it earlier and that now

Renault will have to wait until 2004 to do so.

You may be right, but don't forget that Renault provided the engines that claimed five world championships for Williams and one for Benetton between 1992 and 1997, so they clearly have more than a little expertise on hand.

All right then, so nothing is being given away on that front. So, how about their chassis? Will technical director Mike Gascoyne have orchestrated the troops to good effect to build a chassis that will be able to harness all this extra Renault horsepower?

That's his job.

Flavio said last January at the team's launch that he would be disappointed if Renault didn't rank in the top four in 2002. Do you reckon that the same holds true for the season ahead?

Even more so, I would say.

It seems almost rude to point this out, but Renault's fourth place was still a long way behind Ferrari, Williams and McLaren.

No, it's not rude, as it's a fact, and I hear that Renault is working on it.

JARNO TRULLI

TIME TO DELIVER

This is a make-or-break year for Jarno, as years of promise not being backed up by strong results have started to dent the reputation of this undoubtedly rapid Italian.

Wins Needed: Jarno will use all his speed and famous dedication to chase the results many feel that his mercurial skills deserve.

I f Renault's chassis is better than last year's, which it needs to be, then Jarno will be smiling in the 17 races ahead. If the Renault engine is both more powerful than last year, and more reliable, then he'll be happier still. But, if they're not and he spends another year scrapping for the points, then he'll be gutted, as he was once seen as one of the brightest talents in Formula One – especially when he led the 1997 Austrian GP for Prost – and the lack of a top-line drive has left him scrabbling to land the results that his talents ought to have brought him.

To many, Jarno is an enigma. He's fast all right, outqualifying his 2002 team-mate Jenson Button 12:5, but Button collected more points, allowing many critics to opine that Jarno wasn't tough enough in the races. However, examination of last year's results ought to put the record straight. Jarno was running second behind Coulthard in Melbourne, holding off Michael Schumacher, but spun out. He blasted past the McLarens at Interlagos, but his car failed. Although he struggled at Imola, he was set for points at Barcelona. Finally, his luck came good at Monaco and he raced to fourth, then sixth at Montreal. More mechanical failures and a falling away from the pace by Renault meant that Jarno wasn't to score again for a further seven races, getting back on track at Monza when he overcame dropping to the back of the grid on the parade lap to race to fourth, albeit with both Williams and McLarens out of the running. Fifth at Indianapolis marked continued form.

TRACK NOTES

Nationality	**ITALIAN**
Born	**13 JULY, 1974, PESCARA, ITALY**
Website	**www.jarnotrulli.com**
Teams	**MINARDI 1997, PROST 1997–1999, JORDAN 2000–2001, RENAULT 2003**

CAREER RECORD

First Grand Prix	**1997 AUSTRALIAN GP**
Grand Prix starts	**97**
Grand Prix wins	**0 (best result: second 1999 European GP)**
Poles	**0**
Fastest laps	**0**
Points	**38**
Honours	**1996 GERMAN FORMULA THREE CHAMPION, 1994 WORLD KART CHAMPION**

A karting superstar

Jarno was a trend-setter in leaping from karts to Formula Three. However, with a karting pedigree as blue-chip as Jarno's this wasn't a surprise, for he'd been world champion in 1994. Backed by Flavio Briatore, Jarno started his car career mid-1995. He then won the 1996 German Formula Three title and pronounced himself ready for Formula One. Minardi listened and an 11th-hour deal had him lined up at Melbourne without a test to his name. He was soon faster than team-mate Ukyo Katayama and replaced the injured Olivier Panis at Prost, scoring his first points and leading that Austrian GP. Staying with Prost for the next two years meant he seldom had a competitive car, but he grabbed second in the topsy-turvy 1999 European GP before moving on, in 2000, to Jordan for whom he qualified on the front row at Monaco and Spa-Francorchamps, two real drivers' tracks.

FERNANDO ALONSO

FLAVIO'S FAVOURITE

Here's the driver who has taken Jenson Button's place at Renault. And, for those who've forgotten, Fernando Alonso is quick. Very quick.

TRACK NOTES

Nationality	SPANISH
Born	29 JULY, 1981, OVIEDO, SPAIN
Website	www.fernandoalonso.cjb.net
Teams	MINARDI 2001, RENAULT 2003

CAREER RECORD

First Grand Prix	2001
	AUSTRALIAN GP
Grand Prix starts	17
Grand Prix wins	0
(best result: 10th, 2001 German GP)	
Poles	0
Fastest laps	0
Points	0
Honours	1999 FORMULA NISSAN CHAMPION, 1997 ITALIAN & SPANISH KART CHAMPION, 1996 WORLD & SPANISH KART CHAMPION, 1995 & 1994 SPANISH JUNIOR KART CHAMPION

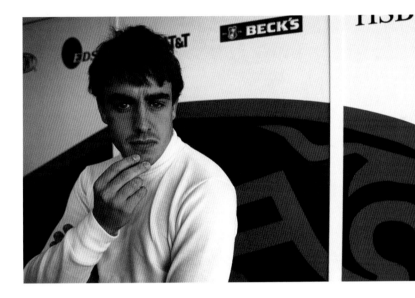

Watch This Face: Fernando is sure to spring a few surprises with Renault in 2003 after a year spent out of the limelight as the team's test driver, getting in valuable mileage for the team.

Fernando arrived in 2001, made an impact and then disappeared from the radar last year, consigned to the invisible ranks of test drivers. And now Fernando's back, still only 21 years old and raring to go, placed at Renault alongside Jarno Trulli by team proprietor Flavio Briatore, who just happens to be his personal manager as well, explaining why Jenson Button has been pushed aside to accommodate him.

However, before people become indignant and state that "Our Jenson" shouldn't have been shown the door,

Fernando is no slouch behind the wheel and will undoubtedly be an asset for Renault. Whether he proves better than Jenson remains to be seen.

Certainly, all but the most eagle-eyed might not have noticed Fernando's progress two summers ago. After all, he was driving for tailenders Minardi, not a team that normally troubles the scorers. Indeed, the team operated on a higher plane in 2002 than it did the year before.

But he was neat, tidy and consistent, scoring a best result of 10th in the German GP. And he was as fast as his machinery

permitted, which is all one could ask of any Formula One rookie. Having shown speed aplenty as Renault developed its car through testing last year, as well as impressing Jaguar when he tested for them last summer, Fernando ought to go well this year. Certainly, if the car is good enough for points he will score them.

Teenaged prodigy

A karting hotshot in his native Spain, winner of multiple national junior championships, Fernando made an instant impact on the international karting scene as soon as he was old enough, becoming world champion. On graduating to car racing in 1999, Fernando was clearly in a hurry, vaulting straight past the junior formulae to race in Spain's Open Fortuna championship, a category with cars almost of Formula 3000 level. And he won that at the first time of asking, racing for a team owned and run by Spanish former Minardi driver

Adrian Campos. Moving on up to the international Formula 3000 championship in 2000, he went better and better, finishing second then first in the final two rounds to rank fourth overall. Not surprisingly, Formula One beckoned and Fernando leapt at the chance to join Minardi. Fernando was partnered by the fast but inconsistent Tarso Marques, outpacing him at will. The gap to Gaston Mazzacane in the final few races was greater still. But then he found himself out of a race seat and, at Flavio's behest, off to test for Renault in 2002.

>> SAUBER

FIGHTING THEIR CORNER

Sauber shocked the establishment by ranking fourth overall in 2001, doing well to drop only one place last year.

The Quiet Man: Peter Sauber doesn't talk a lot, but he simply gets on with the job of running a solidly competitive team on a relatively small budget, as an example to more profilgate others.

Peter Sauber exercised his option on Nick Heidfeld's services fairly early last year. He must be pleased with him?

Yes, he is and so he should be as Nick is a truly excellent racer.

Felipe Massa arrived with the team at the start of last year with precious little experience in top-line racing formulae and it sometimes showed as he threw his car at the scenery. It was great to watch, every lap a different, on-the-edge adjustment. Do you reckon that the team regretted signing such an inexperienced driver?*

Well, they spent a lot of the season trying to smooth the rough edges off his driving, but he's certainly got a lot of natural speed.

Or do you think that it was worth their sticking their neck out to find the stars of tomorrow after their stellar success in unearthing Kimi Raikkonen in 2001?

Kimi proved that it's always worth taking a gamble on a young driver.

It looked to many that Sauber managed to make lightning strike twice, as Felipe was undoubtedly very fast, but he seemed a little, how shall we say, erratic. Is that fair, or not?

Yes, and Sauber certainly hoped that Felipe would be able to be a more consistent challenge to Nick who almost never put a wheel out of line.

There appeared to be some internecine strife at the German GP when Felipe was unhappy at being told to let Nick through in the race. Everyone said that they engaged

FOR THE RECORD

Country of origin:	Switzerland
Team base:	Hinwil, Switzerland
Telephone:	(41) 1937 9000
Website:	www.sauber-petronas.com
Active in Formula One:	From 1993
Grands Prix contested:	164
Wins:	0
Pole positions:	0
Fastest laps:	0

DRIVERS + RESULTS 2002

Driver	Nationality	Races	Wins	Pts	Pos
Nick Heidfeld	German	17	-	7	10th
Felipe Massa	Brazilian	17	-	4	12th

THE TEAM

Team principal:	Peter Sauber
Technical director:	Willy Rampf
Team manager:	Beat Zehnder
Chief designer:	Seamus Mullarkey
Chief engineer:	Jacky Eeckelaert
Test driver:	tba
Chassis:	Sauber C22
Engine:	Petronas Ferrari V10
Tyres:	Bridgestone

in frank discussions with him afterwards?

I'm sure that that's a private matter.

I'll take that as a "no comment" then?

No comment...

Talking of personnel, is it still difficult for Sauber to attract personnel away from the British teams to uproot and settle in Switzerland?

No, but Peter Sauber is extremely bored of such questions. It is possible to run a team from a country other than England you know.

Fair cop, as Ferrari seem to have a fair clue on how it's done...

Indeed they do.

And the engines with which Ferrari supplies Sauber, from the previous season, certainly aren't short on horsepower.

Yes, it's an arrangement with which the team is very happy.

Looking to 2003, there's an all-German driver line-up with Heinz-Harald Frentzen signing to partner Nick. Will this help attract German sponsors?

Perhaps, but, in the current financial climate, sponsorship of any

Computer Games: Two Sauber engineers study the data in their perpetual search for those all-important extra fractions of a second.

kind is welcomed from any source.

Talking of budgetary matters, Sauber seems to be one of the only good, old-fashioned teams where racing comes ahead of the size of the team motorhome. Is this out of choice or expedience, running a tight ship and keeping staff to a bare minimum?

Absolutely. For example, you need a lot of staff to develop the software for the driver aids and Sauber has just one man in this role...

Apart from possibly helping Sauber to land a larger budget, what attracted the team to Heinz-Harald. After all, at 35, he's no spring chicken in age-conscious Formula One?

Quite simply, Sauber knows Heinz-Harald is an excellent driver from when it ran him between 1994 and 1996. In fact, Peter Sauber knows him even from before that, from when he ran him in the Mercedes sportscar team in 1990. So, you could say, he's back among old friends.

Heinz-Harald has said that although he shares a language with the team, he can't always understand all of the mechanics and thus has to converse in English.

Ah yes, some of Sauber's crew speak a Swiss dialect that Heinz-Harald can't understand.

It's not just Heinz-Harald's racing abilities that attract Sauber to this three-time Grand Prix winner, though, is it?

No, as with the experience that he's gained, especially when he spent two years racing with Williams, he's become an excellent development driver.

Once Sauber had signed Heinz-Harald, there was even talk of him racing in the final few races of 2002. Why was that ruled out?

He was too tall to fit into the car...

But then Felipe got a penalty for his driving tactics at Monza that meant that he would be put 10 places back on the grid for the next race, at Indianapolis, Sauber suddenly found a way to make Heinz-Harald fit.

Ah yes, but it was quite a squeeze.

NICK HEIDFELD

Nick is fast becoming one of Formula One's more experienced drivers, which is why the little German is desperate to hit the big time in his third year with Sauber.

Small and unremarkable in appearance, whatever length he grows his hair, Nick is a driver whose racing ought to receive more accolades than it does. The 25-year-old German drives for Sauber, a team that remains almost invisible despite fighting with the like of Renault, Jordan and BAR. However, Nick is a driver who raced to third in Brazil in 2001 and matched or outpaced rookie hotshot Kimi Raikkonen, before the latter got the nod over Nick to race for McLaren. Joined by Felipe Massa – another rookie hotshot – last year, Nick knew that whatever speed Felipe showed he had to not only match it but also emphasise the guile, consistency and experience gained from 50 plus Grands Prix that makes it all the more valuable to a team. He did, and so it was Massa who left the team, and not voluntarily.

For 2003, Heidfeld is joined by compatriot Heinz-Harald Frentzen, who will provide the first real yardstick that Nick has had, since he wasn't overshadowed by Jean Alesi at lacklustre Prost in 2000. By season's end, we'll know if he's as good as many think he is. So, in a way, it's a make-or-break year for Nick.

Looking back at 2002, Nick started well with fifth place in the second race, at Sepang, lost a point to mechanical failure in

Looking Relaxed: Nick is one of only a few drivers in Formula One who always manage to look unruffled, whatever the circumstance.

Brazil, led a Sauber four–five in Spain, but then lost control in Austria and took out Sato. Being beaten to sixth by Massa at the Nurburgring won't have pleased him, but being sixth at Silverstone did. Only one more point, for sixth at Hockenheim, followed.

TRACK NOTES

Nationality	**GERMAN**
Born	**10 MAY, 1977,**
	MOENCHENGLADBACH, GERMANY
Website	**www.nick-heidfeld.de**
Teams	**PROST 2000,**
	SAUBER 2001-2003

CAREER RECORD

First Grand Prix	1999
	AUSTRALIAN GP
Grand Prix starts	51
Grand Prix wins	0 (best result:
	third, 2001 Brazilian GP)
Poles	0
Fastest laps	0
Points	19
Honours	1999 FORMULA 3000
	CHAMPION, 1998 FORMULA 3000
	RUNNER-UP, 1997 GERMAN
	FORMULA THREE CHAMPION, 1995
	GERMAN FORMULA FORD
	CHAMPION, 1994 GERMAN FF1600
	CHAMPION

Much garlanded racer

Winning the German Formula Three title in 1997 to add to his 1995 national Formula Ford title set Nick on the road to the top. Driving for McLaren's junior team in Formula 3000 – while testing their Formula One cars at the behest of Mercedes – he nearly made it two titles in a row, but one small slip let Juan Pablo Montoya take the glory. Bouncing back in 1999, Nick made no mistake and won the title.

Having tested for McLaren for several years, Nick would have loved to step up to the race team, but there were no openings as the Hakkinen/Coulthard axis was going strong, so Nick's break in Formula One in 2000 came with Prost. Trouble was, this was a team in decline, and he did well to score an eighth place, one better than Alesi managed all year. Matters improved once he joined Sauber in 2001.

HEINZ-HARALD FRENTZEN

BACK WHERE HE STARTED

A return to Sauber is something that Heinz-Harald hopes will make him smile again after a couple of troubled seasons have left him anxious to restore his reputation.

After two years in which he left a team before the season was out, with Jordan in 2001 and Arrows in 2002, respectively, Heinz-Harald is banking on a return to his first Formula One team to regain his form. So, seven years after he left Sauber, the German is returning. And it's a team that has gained much valuable experience since he left at the end of 1996 to join Williams. The highlight of his three-year spell with the Swiss team was third place in the 1995 Italian GP.

Not only will this affable German be looking forward to the team's enhanced experience, but he'll also be looking forward to having a ride that will last for all 16 races of the World Championship. He'll feel inspired too that team owner Peter Sauber appreciates his abilities: "To defend fifth place in the championship, you need drivers who're able to score at every event and push each other. And then you have to talk about developing the car. Heinz is not only one of the quickest drivers out there, but he can push a team forwards on the technical side."

Last year was a trial with Arrows, but one with glimpses of promise, as shown at Barcelona where he finished sixth. He was sixth again at Monaco after being fastest in the warm-up. Heinz-Harald even caught the Raikkonen/Barrichello battle, but his hopes of being fourth when they clashed were ruined by a failing fuel rig. By the Hungarian GP, though, he was out of a drive, having quit Arrows. That ought to have been the end of his season, but Heinz-Harald got to race for Sauber sooner than expected, though, standing in for Felipe Massa at Indianapolis when the Brazilian was facing punishment from the FIA.

Nationality	GERMAN
Born	18 MAY, 1967
	MOENCHENGLADBACH, GERMANY
Website	www.hhf.de
Teams	SAUBER 1994–1996,
	2002–2003, WILLIAMS
	1997–1998, JORDAN 1999–2001,
	PROST 2001, ARROWS 2002

CAREER RECORD

First Grand Prix	1994
	BRAZILIAN GP
Grand Prix starts	142
Grand Prix wins	3
	(1997 San Marino GP,
	1999 French GP, Italian GP)
Poles	2
Fastest laps	6
Points	162
Honours	1997 FORMULA
	ONE RUNNER-UP, 1989 GERMAN
	FORMULA THREE RUNNER-UP, 1988
	GERMAN FORMULA OPEL CHAMPION,
	1984 GERMAN JUNIOR KART
	CHAMPION

Voice Of Experience: Heinz-Harald brings speed, experience and a much-needed sense of humour to the Sauber team. No doubt, the Swiss team's financial security will appeal to him...

Faster than Hakkinen

Not a lot of people know this, but Heinz-Harald beat Mika Hakkinen in straight fights twice in 1988, when they met in the Formula Opel Euroseries. He then was pipped to the 1989 German Formula Three title by Karl Wendlinger, finishing equal on points with Michael Schumacher. Formula 3000 and racing sportscars for Mercedes followed, before Heinz-Harald was brought back from Japan by his former sportscar team boss to drive in Formula One in 1994. That boss was Peter Sauber. Qualifying fifth on his debut showed that the combination had potential. Finishing fifth on his second outing confirmed that. It took his move to Williams in 1997 to give Heinz-Harald his break, though, but he scored just one win as team-mate Jacques Villeneuve won seven and the title. Both struggled in 1998, but his move to Jordan for 1999 yielded wins at Magny-Cours and Monza, marking Heinz-Harald's finest year.

>> JORDAN

NEW MOTIVATION

Jordan's Achilles heel last year was its engine. This year there will be no excuses as Ford power has replaced Honda.

Back At The Helm: Eddie Jordan is returning to a hands-on management role in 2003 as he strives to push Jordan to the head of the midfield.

The biggest change for this year must be the arrival of Ford engines in place of those from Honda?

Yup, more power will be most welcome to the cause.

And better reliability too?

Yes, it was increasingly galling as those Hondas kept going pop. Sure, they were succeeding in finding more power, but it's not always so great if it can't guarantee a finish.

Why do you reckon that Jordan terminated their engine deal with Honda one year early?

They must have preferred the shape of the Ford oval... No, seriously, they did this to land a three-year deal with Ford for engines that should take the team back to the front.

Are they free like the Honda engines were, or will Jordan be paying Ford for using the Cosworth RS1 engine?

At first it looked as though Eddie Jordan would be left with a $15m hole in his wallet for this year, but it appears that a somewhat secret deal has been done.

Yet Jaguar Racing boss Niki Lauda said last July that there was zero possibility of Jordan landing a Ford engine deal. It appears that he was somewhat wrong?

It does rather, doesn't it, but there was a lot of politicking going on between Ford in the States and Ford in Europe. Still, it appears that Formula One got the outcome that it wanted.

Jordan went all quiet last autumn when it was unable to go testing as the Ford V10s

wouldn't fit on their 2002 chassis. How much will this have affected them?

Quite a lot, but as long as design director Henri Durand's aerodynamic planning has been accurate and the weather gives them a break in February so that they can conduct effective testing, then... All right, yes it will have affected them, but there was a question over whether Jordan could have afforded all that track time anyway.

Last year was quite a year for Eddie, though, and he had to take the tough decision midway through the year to get mean and streamline the team. Are more job cuts to come?

You never know. It can't have been an easy decision to make, especially with long-standing colleagues who were friends of Eddie's, but it gave the team a chance to refocus.

It also meant that Eddie got his hands back on the tiller.

Yup. It's what he does best.

One of the other strong points of the team must be the driving skills of Giancarlo Fisichella, a driver who would bring a car home in the points if the car was competitive enough.

Absolutely, he's a great little driver, one of the best.

Conversely, Takuma Sato kept the team's panel beaters rather busy last year.

Didn't he just.

How did Jordan curb his "natural enthusiasm"?

They had a little fireside chat, and that seemed to work. The boy is quick, though.

His assault on his team-mate in the Malaysian GP was returned when Giancarlo hit him at the Nurburgring.

Eddie will thank you for reminding him of that.

But it all came right at the final round, with fifth place for Takuma at Suzuka.

Yes, what a result. Did you see the crowd go mad? Furthermore, the two points propelled Jordan past Jaguar to finish the year sixth overall. Not only that, it marked Takuma's coming of age as he outqualified Giancarlo and very few team mates manage that.

It wasn't an altogether successful year, though, but what do you reckon was Jordan's low point?

Not knowing if Takuma was all right when he'd been T-boned by Nick Heidfeld at the Austrian GP.

That was one of the team's bigger damage bills, presumably?

Oh yes.

You spent much of last winter trying to decide the identity of your second driver. Was this solely down to the loss of budget after sponsor Deutsche Post withdrew?

Well that certainly was a major factor …

There was talk of Eddie Irvine returning in place of Takuma.

From Mr Irvine presumably. By early January they still weren't sure.

The Big Man: Back for a second spell with Jordan, founding partner Gary Anderson brings a wealth of experience applied to practical, mechanical savvy.

FOR THE RECORD

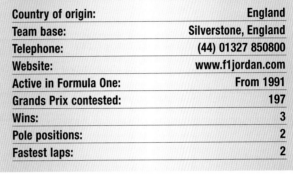

Country of origin:	England
Team base:	Silverstone, England
Telephone:	(44) 01327 850800
Website:	www.f1jordan.com
Active in Formula One:	From 1991
Grands Prix contested:	197
Wins:	3
Pole positions:	2
Fastest laps:	2

DRIVERS + RESULTS 2002

Driver	Nationality	Races	Wins	Pts	Pos
Giancarlo Fisichella	Italian	17	-	7	10th
Takuma Sato	Japanese	17	-	2	15th

THE TEAM

Team principal:	Eddie Jordan
Technical director:	Gary Anderson
Team manager:	Tim Edwards
Chief designer:	Henri Durand
Chief engineer:	Rob Smedley
Test driver:	tba
Chassis:	Jordan EJ13
Engine:	Ford V10
Tyres:	Bridgestone

GIANCARLO FISICHELLA

BETTER AND BETTER

Giancarlo's continued to gild his reputation with a series of storming drives in 2002. With the Ford engine expected to offer more than the Honda did, expect fireworks aplenty in 2003.

Some of Formula One's insiders were heard to voice the opinion last summer that this dapper little Roman was one of the top three drivers. Looking at Giancarlo's run of three fifth places – his best sequence all year – you might have wondered if they had lost their marbles. However, his Jordan was let down by its Honda engine and his persistently strong form suggested that they weren't entirely barmy. Indeed, every team manager he's had speaks highly of him, and they should know. He gets in and gets on with it: fast.

What Giancarlo brings to a team, sheer speed aside, is a cheery demeanour, excellent and accessible media manner, and the will to give it his all. Oh yes, and the experience of having raced in more than 100 Grands Prix. As shown last year, if his car was capable of points, he'd score them. Certainly, none came until the sixth round, when he was fifth at the A1-Ring, but then he repeated this at Monaco and Montreal. Thereafter, a sixth place at the Hungaroring aside, he was snapping away just outside the points, no doubt counting down the days until he is powered by an engine with more power again, for the Honda just wasn't enough to outrace the six cars from the top three teams: Ferrari, Williams and McLaren.

No more points followed, with Giancarlo no doubt anxious simply to get on with 2003.

One Of The Best: Giancarlo has all the skills to be a Grand Prix winner, but has not yet enjoyed a suitable car with which to prove it.

TRACK NOTES

Nationality	**ITALIAN**
Born	**14 JANUARY, 1973,**
	ROME, ITALY
Website	**www.giancarlofisichella.it**
Teams	**MINARDI 1996,**
	JORDAN 1997 & 2002–2003,
	BENETTON 1998–2001

CAREER RECORD

First Grand Prix	**1996**
	AUSTRALIAN GP
Grand Prix starts	**108**
Grand Prix wins	**0 (best result:**
	second, 1997 Belgian GP,
1998 Monaco GP & Canadian GP,	
1999 Canadian GP, 2000 Brazilian GP)	
Poles	**1**
Fastest laps	**1**
Points	**82**
Honours	**1994**
	ITALIAN FORMULA THREE
CHAMPION & MONACO FORMULA	
THREE WINNER, 1991 EUROPEAN	
	KART RUNNER-UP

A Monaco winner

As with almost every single driver in Formula One, Giancarlo was a multi-titled kart racer, peaking with second place in the 1991 European championship. He did well on his graduation to Formula Alfa Boxer that year and, after being runner-up in the Italian Formula Three series in 1993, won the title in 1994. That year, he also made his name by winning the international Formula Three race supporting the Monaco GP. A lack of cash thwarted his ascent to Formula 3000, but Alfa Romeo snapped him up to race touring cars. He raced impressively, right at the front, and in 1996 was offered his Formula One break by Minardi, albeit being dropped to make way for Tarso Marques and Giovanni Lavaggi when the team needed money. Signed by Jordan in 1997, he was running second in Argentina when taken out by team-mate Ralf Schumacher but peaked with second in the German GP. Managed by Flavio Briatore, his mentor took him to Benetton in 1998 where he continued his run of claiming second place finishes, albeit being made to struggle in 2001 when the team spent the year developing Renault's wide-angle engine.

JORDAN No. 2 DRIVER

COME IN NUMBER TWO!

Financial uncertainty meant that Jordan took a while to chose its second driver, with Eddie Irvine, Felipe Massa and Jos Verstappen heading the queue.

The loss of Deutsche Post as team sponsor left Jordan short of budget as it faced up to 2003. Already more streamlined than it had been going into 2002, the team had to consider the wishes of remaining sponsor Benson & Hedges in its choice of a second driver to line up alongside Giancarlo Fisichella, with B&H known to want a British driver.

This made Eddie Irvine favourite to rejoin the team for which he raced from 1993 to 1995 after a torrid time with Jaguar. His outspoken nature would certainly fit the bill as far as B&H was concerned. They want a

driver with profile. However, his wage bill was expected to be more than the team might chose to afford and three other British drivers were mentioned in connection with the second seat once Takuma Sato was confirmed as leaving to become test driver for BAR. Anthony Davidson was at the head of the list. However, two British drivers who had been racing in Japan, both in Formula Nippon and GTs, came into the frame: namely, Ralph Firman and Richard Lyons.

Formula One experience and a budget to go with it, however, made Felipe Massa and Jos Verstappen attractive options.

Red Bull Money

Dietrich Mateschitz, owner of the Red Bull energy drinks company, has long been sniffing around taking over a team after a long relationship with Sauber and, latterly, with Arrows. However, his dream has been to create an American team for American drivers to help him capture the American market. This isn't set to happen just yet, but buying a controlling interest in Jordan suddenly became an option and this potentially opened the door for his regular driver Enrique Bernoldi to step up to join Fisichella.

Yet, as we reached the New Year, no deal had been done, with Sauber reject Felipe Massa convinced that he would be the driver whose name would be on the side of the second Jordan, but Irvine remained as the favourite.

This Is The Target: Whoever signs for the second Jordan seat will have a mountain to climb just to beat team-mate Fisichella.

>> JAGUAR

THE ONLY WAY IS UP

It's been all change at Jaguar since last season with two new bosses and two new drivers.

All Change: With Niki Lauda having been moved aside and replaced as team supremo by Tony Purnell, the everyday running of Jaguar Racing will be in the hands of fellow newcomer David Pitchforth.

FOR THE RECORD

Country of origin:	England
Team base:	Milton Keynes, England
Telephone:	(44) 01908 279700
Website:	www.jaguar-racing.com
Active in Formula One:	From 1997 (as Stewart)
Grands Prix contested:	100
Wins:	1
Pole positions:	1
Fastest laps:	0

DRIVERS + RESULTS 2002

Driver	Nationality	Races	Wins	Pts	Pos
Eddie Irvine	N. Irish	17	-	8	9th
Pedro de la Rosa	Spanish	17	-	-	N/A

THE TEAM

Team principal:	Tony Purnell
Managing director:	David Pitchforth
Technical director:	tba
Chief aerodynamicist:	Ben Agathangelou
Chief designer:	Rob Taylor
Chief engineer:	Malcolm Oastler
Test driver:	tba
Chassis:	Jaguar R4
Engine:	Jaguar V10
Tyres:	Michelin

Let's not beat about the bush. Jaguar Racing had a poor season last year, saved only really by a surprise third place in the Italian GP. Could this season be any worse?

They must be praying not, even though parent company Ford said that they were behind them.

Mind you, lots of football club chairmen say that and then the manager is seen packing his bags the following week.

Quite. And especially so when the world economy is on the downward slope.

Stability is said to be one of the keys to success, as shown by McLaren over the years. But this surely can't be banked on at Jaguar after a season as poor as last year?

Probably not, and close season changes from the top down showed that Ford felt that it was more than the design team that needed change.

Yes, but that was pretty wholesale, wasn't it, with Steve Nichols leaving just before the first race of last season, then Ben Agathangelou joining, then Rob Taylor moving across from Arrows

to replace John Russell. Even BAR's Malcolm Oastler was brought in to help. Was there anyone left?

Er, I'm not sure.

Then there was the small matter of Niki Lauda being replaced by Tony Purnell and Gunther Steiner being realigned to make way for David Pitchforth.

Yup, the changes were comprehensive.

For all the mid-season chassis changes, they took quite a while to propel Jaguar back into the midfield, and even then the form was spasmodic. Why?

The team didn't have the experience in our personnel to unlock the car's potential.

Just when the threat of Ford pulling the plug hung over the team, at the Belgian GP, new front suspension and aero parts were introduced. And they worked.

Huge sighs of relief all round as Eddie Irvine claimed a point after an excellent drive.

MARK WEBBER

ENTERING THE BIG TIME

If Mark can make the same impact that he made in last year's opening race, on home soil in Australia, he'll be doing very well in his first campaign with Jaguar.

CAREER RECORD

First Grand Prix	2002 AUSTRALIAN GP
Grand Prix starts	16
Grand Prix wins	0 (best result: fifth, 2002 Australian GP)
Poles	0
Fastest laps	0
Points	2
Honours	2001 FORMULA 3000 RUNNER-UP, 1998 FIA GT RUNNER-UP, 1996 BRITISH FORMULA FORD RUNNER-UP & FORMULA FORD FESTIVAL WINNER

Jaguar's new signing is a driver in a hurry. Professional in every aspect of his approach, this gung-ho athlete is typically Australian, with that will to win and the confidence and application to make this happen, turning possible defeat into victory.

When Mark romped home a surprise fifth for Formula One's tailenders Minardi after the destruction derby that was his Grand Prix debut in his native Australia, the nation wanted more. Trouble was, that was as good as it got. However, other strong drives convinced many that Mark has a bright future. There were times when he should have been dropped by those in the midfield, but he hung on and peaked with eighth in the French GP. But it was when Mark was eighth fastest in practice at Monaco that he really showed his class. He must be praying that Jaguar can offer him the chance of racing higher up the order.

ANTONIO PIZZONIA

JUNGLE BOY SWINGS IN

CAREER RECORD

First Grand Prix	2003 AUSTRALIAN GP
Grand Prix starts	0
Grand Prix wins	0
Poles	0
Fastest laps	0
Points	0
Honours	2000 BRITISH FORMULA THREE CHAMPION, 1999 BRITISH FORMULA RENAULT CHAMPION, 1998 BRITISH FORMULA RENAULT WINTER SERIES CHAMPION, 1998 BRITISH FORMULA VAUXHALL JUNIOR CHAMPION, 1997 BRITISH FORMULA VAUXHALL JUNIOR WINTER SERIES CHAMPION, 1996 BRAZILIAN KART CHAMPION, 1994, 1993 & 1992 PAULISTA JUNIOR KART CHAMPION

Antonio is new to Formula One, but he already knows about driving a Grand Prix car very quickly.

Antonio attended all of 2002's Grands Prix in Europe for two reasons. Firstly, he was racing in the Formula 3000 support races and, secondly, he would slip into the Formula One paddock and spend time with Williams as one of the team's two test drivers – alongside Marc Gene. Teamed with second-year driver Mark Webber, Antonio actually has more Formula One mileage under his belt, as Mark scarcely tested for Minardi last year, while Antonio was putting in lap after lap for Williams, often matching the pace of the team's racers Juan Pablo Montoya and Ralf Schumacher.

No wonder Jaguar was so keen to sign him. Jaguar wanted some young blood in its line-up for 2003 instead of Eddie Irvine and Pedro de la Rosa. Now it's up to this duo to perform. Although Antonio did not win in Formula 3000 last year, he showed great pace in testing which suggested that he was merely having trouble readjusting to Formula 3000's limited power and grip. Whatever, his endless wins in the junior categories show that he has what it takes.

>> BAR

IN HONDA'S HANDS

Master And Pupil: David Richards has great plans for Jenson Button.

Being the focus of Honda's attention might help BAR move back up the order after a disappointing 2002. That and some inspired management.

FOR THE RECORD

Country of origin:	England
Team base:	Brackley, England
Telephone:	(44) 01280 844212
Website:	www.britishamericanracing.com
	or www.bar.net
Active in Formula One:	From 1999
Grands Prix contested:	67
Wins:	0
Pole positions:	0
Fastest laps:	0

DRIVERS + RESULTS 2002

Driver	Nationality	Races	Wins	Pts	Pos
Olivier Panis	French	17	-	3	14th
Jacques Villeneuve	Canadian	17	-	4	12th

THE TEAM

Team principal:	David Richards
Technical director:	Geoff Willis
Team manager:	Ron Meadows
Chief engineer:	James Robinson
Test drivers:	Anthony Davidson, Takuma Sato
Chassis:	BAR 005
Engine:	Honda V10
Tyres:	Bridgestone

There was talk of BAR being renamed for 2003 but it hasn't happened. Why not?

They couldn't come up with a good enough name. Someone even suggested Dalarna, which team principal David Richards thought sounded like a washing-up liquid.

Renaming apart, everything appears to be more settled and streamlined now that David has had a year at the helm.

Indeed it does.

People say that he's a specialist at taking a long-term view.

Judging by the multifarious successes of his Prodrive engineering company in rallying, touring car and even sportscar racing, you'd have to say that they're right. This approach is also essential if a team is to be in a position to attract top quality staff.

Is it true that BAR will no longer focus on Jacques Villeneuve?

The team was built around him, but this might be starting to change.

Will this upset Jacques?

No, in truth, Jacques will probably relish it, as he's not the sort who needs to be mollycoddled.

For 2003, BAR have exclusive use of Honda engines now that Jordan has fitted Fords, will that help?

They'll hope so, but BAR needs all the help they can get to find those missing horsepower relative to the leading teams.

Reliability wasn't a strong point either in 2002, with Olivier Panis failing to finish a race until round eight.

Yes, reliability was certainly addressed through last year.

On the chassis front, the 005 will be the first BAR that Geoff Willis will have designed. This ought to bolster the team.

It should do, as his record with Williams shows that he can do it.

Richards has been talking of building towards long-term goals. Is this just a clever way of moving the target further away to take the pressure off the team?

It could be, but the team are doing their best to put all the bricks in place for a successful future.

Talking of which, snapping up Jenson Button from Renault was something of a coup.

Richards says that Jenson is a potential world champion.

JACQUES VILLENEUVE

LOOKING FOR MOTIVATION

CAREER RECORD

First Grand Prix	1996
	AUSTRALIAN GP
Grand Prix starts	116
Grand Prix wins	11
(1996 European GP, British GP, Hungarian GP, Portuguese GP, 1997 Brazilian GP, Argentinian GP, Spanish GP, British GP, Hungarian GP, Austrian GP, Luxembourg GP)	
Poles	13
Fastest laps	9
Points	213
Honours	1997 FORMULA ONE CHAMPION, 1996 FORMULA ONE RUNNER-UP, 1995 INDYCAR CHAMPION & INDY 500 WINNER, 1994 INDYCAR ROOKIE OF THE YEAR, 1993 TOYOTA ATLANTIC ROOKIE OF THE YEAR, 1992 JAPANESE FORMULA THREE RUNNER-UP

Jacques starts his fifth year with BAR, desperate for the team to advance from the midfield.

Jacques was rumoured to be heading to race Indycars this year, disillusioned with Formula One, but he's staying on, pledging to give it everything in an attempt to score points on a regular rather than an occasional basis. Indeed, if Honda can offer more power than in 2002 and designer Geoff Willis's first BAR chassis is as good as those he used to pen for Williams, then Jacques might find a way to smile again.

Last year didn't start well for Jacques. Indeed, he started it reeling when friend and mentor Craig Pollock was ousted from the helm of BAR as David Richards took control.

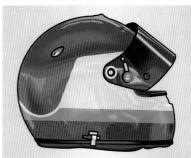
However, with no choice but to get on with it, that's what Jacques did.

Mechanical failure robbed Jacques of points in a race of attrition at Melbourne. He finally scored at Silverstone with a fourth place after great pitstops (and Bridgestone rubber) as others floundered on the dry/wet track and he hit form to be sixth at Indianapolis.

JENSON BUTTON

ALL CHANGE FOR JENSON

CAREER RECORD

First Grand Prix	2000
	AUSTRALIAN GP
Grand Prix starts	51
Grand Prix wins	0
(best result: fourth, 2000 German GP, 2002 Malaysian GP & 2002 Brazilian GP)	
Poles	0
Fastest laps	0
Points	14
Honours	1999 MACAU FORMULA THREE RUNNER-UP, 1998 FORMULA FORD FESTIVAL WINNER & BRITISH FORMULA FORD CHAMPION, 1998 McLAREN AUTOSPORT BRDC YOUNG DRIVER, 1997 EUROPEAN SUPER A KART CHAMPION, 1991 BRITISH CADET KART CHAMPION

It's Jenson's fourth year in Formula One, and he's joining his third team: BAR, with a multi-year contract.

Jenson lost his drive with Renault last year through no fault of his own. There was nothing that he did on track that should have earned his contract not being renewed for 2003. His only crime, it seems, is his choice of management. Or, more to the point, the fact that his career isn't managed by Flavio Briatore, proprietor of Renault Sport.

However, he may have fallen on his feet as David Richards has shown his eye for talent and signed him on a four-year deal,

which is great for Jenson, who'll probably find that extra little bit more now that he feels wanted again. On top of this, there's the factor of BAR enjoying sole relationship with Honda, an engine supplier chastened by its poor showing in 2002.

>> MINARDI

Everyone loves Minardi, the plucky, privately-owned Anglo-Italian team that tries to stick it to the big-hitting manufacturers.

Still Smiling: Paul Stoddart continues to smile in the face of adversity.

FOR THE RECORD

Country of origin:	Italy
Team base:	Faenza, Italy, and Ledbury, England
Telephone:	(39) 0546 696111
Website:	www.minardi.it
Active in Formula One:	From 1985
Grands Prix contested:	288
Wins:	0
Pole positions:	0
Fastest laps:	0

DRIVERS + RESULTS 2002

Driver	Nationality	Races	Wins	Pts	Pos
Anthony Davidson	English	2	-	-	N/A
Mark Webber	Australian	17	-	2	15th
Alex Yoong	Malaysian	15	-	-	N/A

THE TEAM

Team principal:	Paul Stoddart
Technical director:	Gabriele Tredozi
Team manager:	John Walton
Chief designer:	Loic Bigois
Chief engineer:	Andrew Tilley
Test drivers:	Sergey Zlobin, Matteo Bobbi
Chassis:	Minardi PS03
Engine:	Cosworth V10
Tyres:	Michelin

Last year was quite a roller-coaster ride, with financial controversy from the very first round?

Yup, you can say that again.

How secure is Minardi financially for 2003?

That would be telling, but team principal Paul Stoddart and his colleagues should have enough money to last the season.

Should?

Well, you never know when something might blow up in your face.

They've lost Mark Webber to Jaguar. Will Minardi always continue to be a stepping stone for young drivers?

Probably, but it would be great if they were able to keep hold of the better ones. However, that takes money.

Alex Yoong brought money but no particular pace in 2002. Will this always be the fate of teams like Minardi, having to pick a driver for the size of his wallet?

Economics are economics, so there's always a chance that at least one of the drivers will need to arrive with a fat briefcase.

Justin Wilson brought a couple of million.

Yup, and he also brings acknowledged speed, so he could be a major attribute. Indeed, Stoddart certainly thinks that he will be.

Is it true that there were 20 drivers vying for the second seat even before last season was over?

Yup, the Minardi motorhome had to have a revolving door fitted...

Asiatech engines powered the Minardis last year. What's under the bonnet this time around?

Ford Cosworth engines, the most competitive they've had in 19 years.

Are the team having to dip into their budget for these?

Sadly, it seems they are, meaning that their budget has to be close on that of the midfield teams who are lucky enough to have works engine deals.

Streuth! There was talk in 2002 of Minardi trying to land an engine deal with Ferrari, something like Sauber has.

Yes, but that would still have cost money. Lots of money, in fact.

JUSTIN WILSON

Justin was thought to be too tall for a Formula One car, but Minardi has made an extra long cockpit in order to make him fit.

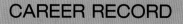

Justin has made it to Formula One on merit, being the first driver announced by the Anglo-Italian team last December. It cost him and his mentor Jonathan Palmer £2m that will have to be repaid to their future backers, but you get the feeling the team principal Paul Stoddart would have moved heaven and earth to sign him anyhow. You see, Stoddart feels that in Justin he has another driver who will go places, like last year's team leader Mark Webber. Indeed, Justin could be better still, as last time they raced together, in 2001, the tall Yorkshireman put one over the Aussie to win the Formula 3000 title.

Justin ought to have made his Formula One debut standing in for Alex Yoong at Minardi last summer. However, as has been much documented, his 6ft 3in stature was too much for the cockpit. Anxious to have him, Stoddart made sure that the 2003 Minardi was longer in the cockpit.

Justin made an immediate impression when he had his first car race in the Formula Vauxhall Junior in 1994 at the age of 16. He finished third overall in 1995, advancing as he gained experience to notch up four race wins. Moving up to slicks and wings in Formula Vauxhall in 1996, Justin was runner-up, but he came good to win the Formula Palmer Audi title in 1998, landing a seat in Formula 3000 for 1999 as part of his prize. Fast from the outset in this category, he scored points for Astromega, then became a frontrunner for Nordic in 2000 before taking three wins to dominate all before him in 2001 to waltz to the title and truly merit his elevation to Formula One.

TRACK NOTES

Nationality	ENGLISH
Born	JULY 31, 1978, SHEFFIELD, ENGLAND
Website	www.justinwilson.com
Teams	MINARDI 2003

CAREER RECORD

First Grand Prix	2003 AUSTRALIAN GP
Grand Prix starts	0
Grand Prix wins	0
Poles	0
Fastest laps	0
Points	0
Honours	2001 FORMULA 3000 CHAMPION; 1998 FORMULA PALMER AUDI CHAMPION; 1996 FORMULA VAUXHALL RUNNER-UP

JOS VERSTAPPEN

This Flying Dutchman looked to be forever on Formula One's scrapheap, but he'll be out to prove everyone wrong by trying to propel Minardi towards the points.

It was acknowledged throughout the Formula One paddock that Jos Verstappen had had his day. It wasn't that he wasn't fast enough for racing's big time, as he is. It was just that he'd found himself on the sidelines when Arrows failed to honour a contract with him for 2002. That and the perpetual raft of young hotshots turning up, and the diminishing number of race seats as teams continue to fall by the wayside. So it was with surprise and delight, as he's a popular, unassuming figure,

that it became clear late last summer that Jos was to lead Minardi in 2003. The Dutch racing fans were delighted, as they'd started to lose interest without one of their own to cheer on.

But as autumn turned to winter, his ride became questionable, indeed compatriot Christijan Albers moved ahead of him in a long list of drivers who were chasing the second Minardi ride once Justin Wilson had been the first driver confirmed by the team. Amid all this uncertainty, it seemed that Jos's management

team didn't feel that a driver of his calibre should have to bring a budget. However, as it happens, some Dutch backers were interested if Jos got the drive and so he was duly named early in January.

Now that the dust has settled, look for more "Jos the boss" banners trackside in 2003. With his wealth of experience, Jos should be the ideal team-mate to guide Formula One rookie Wilson in Minardi's other seat. And, with Ford power, he may yet pull off a surprise or two.

Jos swept through the junior formulae, winning the German Formula Three title before stunning more experienced drivers when he proved right on the pace in a test for Footwork. Snapped up by Benetton as test driver for 1994, he got his chance when JJ Lehto was sidelined with a broken neck. Two third places were the highlight, being burned around the face in a pitfire at Hockenheim the nadir.

Jos was dropped at the end of the year, then raced for Simtek, Arrows, Tyrrell and Stewart between 1995 and 1998, before rejoining Arrows in 2000 and staying for two years.

>> TOYOTA

MOVING UP A GEAR

Mr O: Ove Andersson is being allowed to focus on Formula One in 2003.

Well-funded Toyota should start to accelerate up the order this year after a debut season that yielded just two points.

FOR THE RECORD

Country of origin:	Germany
Team base:	Cologne, Germany
Telephone:	(49) 2234 18230
Website:	www.toyota-f1.com
Active in Formula One:	2002
Grands Prix contested:	17
Wins:	0
Pole positions:	0
Fastest laps:	0

DRIVERS + RESULTS 2002

Driver	Nationality	Races	Wins	Pts	Pos
Allan McNish	Scottish	16	-	-	N/A
Mika Salo	Finnish	17	-	2	15th

CAR SPECIFICATIONS

Team principal:	Ove Andersson
Technical director:	Dago Roehrer
Team manager:	Ange Pasquali
Chief designer:	Gustav Brunner
Chief engineer:	Humphrey Corbett
Test driver:	Ricardo Zonta
Chassis:	Toyota TF103
Engine:	Toyota V10
Tyres:	Michelin

Was a point in Toyota's first race, last year's Australian GP, something of a false dawn?

No, just a nice welcome for the Japanese newcomers.

But in 2001, team boss Ove Andersson had talked of being happy just to qualify for races in 2002.

That was his first aim, but he also said that he wanted Toyota to gain the respect of the other teams. I think that they achieved that.

It's always said that a team's second year in Formula One is harder than its first, as they spend so much of that first year focusing on each race as it comes that they forget to focus enough on the following season. Should they be concerned about this?

Maybe, as previously Jordan and Stewart struggled thus.

What steps have Toyota taken to ensure they buck this trend?

Gustav Brunner was working on the 2003 car from mid-season.

Horsepower didn't appear to be a problem, with Toyota's engine pushing out more than the Mercedes, Honda and Renault units last year. Should we expect even more in 2003?

Bet your last dollar on it.

It looked as though Mika Salo and Allan McNish did a good job in 2002. Any idea why were they dropped?

Toyota appeared to want some fresh thinking. But it's most unusual to cast aside both as you lose your frame of reference.

Olivier Panis will certainly do a great job for Toyota.

Yes, as he's fast, technical and unfussy.

What of second signing Cristiano da Matta? He won last year's ChampCar title, but he has no knowledge of Formula One.

Actually, he tested for Toyota and went well, but he didn't exactly set the world alight when he last raced in Europe, in Formula 3000 in 1996.

Testing mileage is everything to a young team. Is this why Toyota are planning to run a pair of test teams in 2003?

Precisely.

A second test team is a luxury for which the midfield teams would give their eye teeth.

You bet. In fact, they'd give them even for *one* test team...

One of the keys to the accuracy of the feedback is to have experienced drivers, and yet Toyota have re-signed Ryan Briscoe, who has never raced in Formula One.

Yes, but Ryan gained valuable track time when testing during 2002.

OLIVIER PANIS

VALUED EXPERIENCE

Toyota shocked everyone in the paddock by sacking both drivers at the end of last year, but everyone approves of their signing of Olivier.

Nationality	FRENCH
Born	2 SEPTEMBER, 1966, LYON, FRANCE
Website	www.olivier-panis.com
Teams	LIGIER/PROST 1994–1999, BAR 2001–2002, TOYOTA 2003

CAREER RECORD

First Grand Prix	1994 BRAZILIAN GP
Grand Prix starts	125
Grand Prix wins	1 (1996 Monaco GP)
Poles	0
Fastest laps	0
Points	64
Honours	1993 FORMULA 3000 CHAMPION, 1991 FRENCH FORMULA THREE RUNNER-UP, 1989 FRENCH FORMULA RENAULT CHAMPION

Olivier Panis will never be a fashionable face in the Formula One paddock. He's not flashy enough for that, caring little for the accoutrements of his fellow millionaires. But those who run the teams know full well that Olivier brings undoubted speed: you don't outpace a team-mate as rapid as Jacques Villeneuve without it. He's also an excellent development driver and a real team player, the sort of driver who earns his crew's devotion by simply getting on with the job in hand and doing it well. Toyota need these virtues, as the loss of continuity with the departure of both Mika Salo and Allan McNish after the team's first season won't help their development one little bit. Indeed, with Toyota conducting much of its testing at the Paul Ricard circuit, it gives Olivier an excuse to base himself in the South of France, something that appeals to this most French of drivers.

Poor mechanical reliability at BAR cost him dear in 2002, and he didn't even finish a race until the eighth round, when he came home eighth in Canada. Then, apart from a fifth place finish at Silverstone and a sixth place at Monza, Olivier struggled like all other users of Honda engines, as they offered little in the way of power and even less in the way of reliability. In fact, if there was a mechanical failure to be had, it would inevitably be Olivier who would be left walking back to the pits. Oh how his patience must have been tried.

CRISTIANO DA MATTA

TRACK NOTES

CHAMPION FROM OVER THERE

ChampCar champion last year, Cristiano da Matta has made his long wished-for jump to Formula One, alongside Olivier Panis at Toyota.

Nationality	BRAZILIAN
Born	19 SEPTEMBER, 1973, BELO HORIZONTE, BRAZIL
Website	www.damatta.com
Teams	TOYOTA 2003

CAREER RECORD

First Grand Prix	2003 AUSTRALIAN GP
Grand Prix starts	0
Grand Prix wins	0
Poles	0
Fastest laps	0
Points	0
Honours	2002 CHAMPCAR CHAMPION, 1998 INDY LIGHTS CHAMPION, 1994 BRAZILIAN FORMULA THREE CHAMPION, 1993 BRAZILIAN FORMULA FORD CHAMPION, 1991 BRAZILIAN KARTING CHAMPION

One of the most intriguing sights of 2003 is going to be how Cristiano da Matta fares in the second Toyota. The tiny Brazilian arrives armed with the ChampCar title, but recently only Jacques Villeneuve and Juan Pablo Montoya have made this move successfully before, whereas others such as Alessandro Zanardi and Michael Andretti have failed. And, looking at his racing career to date, Cristiano is nowhere near as garlanded as the tragic Italian.

There is no doubting that Cristiano is a tidy driver, intelligent enough to make the most of the equipment at hand. But the question remains about the comparative level of driving skills in ChampCars which appears to have slipped ever further behind Formula One in the past few seasons.

BRITISH DRIVERS IN FORMULA 1

NATIONAL PRIDE

The search for the next British World Champion is on. Will it be one of the current crop in racing's big time? Or will this honour fall to a driver not yet known in international circles?

Different times: Double World Champion Graham Hill enjoys a celebratory drink after another win in his lengthy Grand Prix career.

A glance at the record books reveals that British drivers are at the top of the tree when it comes to winning the Formula One World Championship. Mike Hawthorn, Graham Hill, Jim Clark, John Surtees, Jackie Stewart, James Hunt, Nigel Mansell and Damon Hill share 12 of the 53 world titles between them. The Brazilians are next on eight. And the Italians? They're not even in the hunt, with their most recent title coming when Alberto Ascari made it two on the trot all the way back in 1953. Yet what is the chance one of today's British Formula One stars or one of the hotshots following in their wheeltracks adding to Britain's tally in the future?

Former ITV commentator Murray Walker said in 1999 that there wasn't an obvious flier on the way up and that Britain was in danger of having no representation at all should David Coulthard and Eddie Irvine retire from Formula One. Fortunately, Jenson Button exceeded all expectations and vaulted past Formula 3000 to land a ride with Williams for 2000, but we can't be sure that those following him will be so fortunate. Indeed, with only 10 teams contesting Formula One these days, there are thus just 20 drives up for grabs, and many of these are filled by drivers on multi-year contracts.

In fact, getting into Formula One is the hardest part of all. Take Coulthard, who is

Our Lionheart: Nigel Mansell fought against the odds to reach Formula One, but his perseverance paid off when he came good in his 12th year.

staying for an eighth year with McLaren. He made the leap into the big time only courtesy of graduating from Williams' test team on Ayrton Senna's death. Irvine was a late-season replacement, chosen for his knowledge of Suzuka. Button's leap from Formula Three to Formula One with Williams in 2000 was a positive selection, coming as a result of his speed in testing rather than jingoism by the team principals. For 2003, he has BAR right behind him, as shown by boss David Richards who said: "a young British driver is a motivational thing for a young British-based team." And so it should be.

The biggest problem that aspiring drivers face is catching the eye of the team principals and, with an explosion of junior formulae, there's no longer an obvious ladder to the top as the old route via Formula Three and Formula 3000 is no longer the only way. So, those team principals have to throw their nets a little wider, with the cast of aspiring hotshots spread thinly over Formula 3000, Formula Nippon, Formula Nissan and even Toyota Atlantic, making comparison difficult once they've graduated from Formula Three. And, as a result, some drivers find it hard to get themselves recognized in the hierarchy.

While Formula 3000 heads the support programme at most Grands Prix, the principals of the tail-end Formula One teams are often more receptive to an inferior driver with a big cheque. With only 20 possible seats, their chances are increasingly limited. To make matters worse, even those who break in can struggle to impress if they're held back by uncompetitive and unreliable machinery. It's a far cry from the 1970s when a team could buy a Ford DFV engine, build a car and run in the knowledge that their drivers weren't faced with a 100bhp deficit. If a driver had talent, it showed. Indeed, it's unlikely Britain's three most recent world champions – James Hunt, Nigel Mansell and Damon Hill – would have become world champions if they'd started with a tail-end team today. Hesketh, an ailing Lotus and a soon-to-fold Brabham gave them just enough of a chance to show their speed, and the rest is history.

Anxious to gain admission is Justin Wilson who showed Mark Webber how it should be done when beating him to the 2001 Formula 3000 title. It appeared that his 6ft 3in stature would prove too great for any of the cars in Formula One, until Minardi designed their 2003 car to accommodate him. In December, Wilson signed for the Anglo-Italian team

Anthony Davidson – Takuma Sato's sparring partner in Formula Three in 2001 – spent last year testing for BAR and showed his skills when all but matching Webber on two outings for Minardi late in the season. However, with no seat in the offing, he's expected either to race in the CART series or to continue as test driver for another year.

With a lack of money from British industry, there were no British drivers with a regular Formula 3000 drive last year. So talent spotters had to look to Formula Three. Robbie Kerr won last year's British Formula Three title, while compatriot Gary Paffett was German Formula Three Champion.

Best placed from the ranks of British drivers, though, is Ralph Firman, who won the Formula Nippon title in 2002. British Formula Three champion in 1996, when Juan Pablo Montoya ranked only fifth, it's high time he was given a shot, at least as a test driver. Trouble is, he, like Wilson, stands well over six foot tall.

A Spent Force?: Since moving from frontrunning Ferrari to midfield Jaguar at the end of 1999, Eddie Irvine has lost his chance to go for gold.

McLaren makes the most effort in bringing British drivers along, having run a scholarship since 1989, numbering Coulthard and Button among its scholars. Commendably, ITV commentator Martin Brundle is heavily involved in this, as he's a bigshot at the British Racing Drivers' Club, joint backers of this annual scholarship. McLaren has also involved itself with karting, backing the leading British championships, and it was through this that it snapped up Lewis Hamilton. He's just finished his first year of car racing, as a winner in British and European Formula Renault, and faces more of the same in 2003, as McLaren guides him up through the ranks. For all this support, though, Coulthard famously asked: "Can we manufacture talent? No, you've either got it or you haven't." A little assistance would surely not go amiss, though.

So, have we cause to expect a British world champion in the future? Only time will tell.

A Long Time Coming: Allan McNish took many years to reach Formula One, then was dropped.

BRITISH DRIVERS IN FORMULA ONE

Year	Races	British Drivers	Winners	Wins	Champion (Best finish)
1950	7	9	0	0	(Reg Parnell/Peter Whitehead 9th)
1951	8	10	0	0	(Reg Parnell 10th)
1952	8	21	0	0	(Mike Hawthorn 4th)
1953	9	18	1	1	(Mike Hawthorn 4th)
1954	9	17	0	0	(Mike Hawthorn 3rd)
1955	7	12	1	1	(Stirling Moss 2nd)
1956	8	14	2	2	(Stirling Moss 2nd)
1957	8	14	2	3*	(Stirling Moss 2nd)
1958	11	14	4	9	**Mike Hawthorn**
1959	9	19	2	4	(Tony Brooks 2nd)
1960	10	20	1	2	(Stirling Moss 3rd)
1961	8	18	2	3	(Stirling Moss 3rd)
1962	9	10	2	7	**Graham Hill**
1963	10	12	3	10	**Jim Clark**
1964	10	11	3	7	**John Surtees**
1965	10	12	3	9	**Jim Clark**
1966	9	13	3	4	(John Surtees 2nd)
1967	11	13	2	5	(Jim Clark 3rd)
1968	12	13	3	7	**Graham Hill**
1969	11	10	2	7	**Jackie Stewart**
1970	13	8	1	1	(Jackie Stewart 5th)
1971	11	12	2	7	**Jackie Stewart**
1972	12	9	1	4	(Jackie Stewart 2nd)
1973	15	11	1	5	**Jackie Stewart**
1974	15	13	0	0	(James Hunt 8th)
1975	14	13	1	1	(James Hunt 4th)
1976	16	6	2	7	**James Hunt**
1977	17	8	1	3	(James Hunt 5th)
1978	16	3	0	0	(John Watson 6th)
1979	15	3	0	0	(John Watson 9th)
1980	14	5	0	0	(John Watson 10th)
1981	15	5	1	1	(John Watson 6th)
1982	16	6	1	2	(John Watson 2nd)
1983	15	6	1	1	(John Watson 6th)
1984	16	4	0	0	(Derek Warwick 7th)
1985	16	6	1	2	(Nigel Mansell 6th)
1986	16	5	1	5	(Nigel Mansell 2nd)
1987	16	4	1	6	(Nigel Mansell 2nd)
1988	16	5	0	0	(Derek Warwick 7th)
1989	16	6	1	2	(Nigel Mansell 4th)
1990	16	4	1	1	(Nigel Mansell 5th)
1991	16	4	1	5	(Nigel Mansell 2nd)
1992	16	4	1	9	**Nigel Mansell**
1993	16	6	1	3	(Damon Hill 3rd)
1994	16	7	2	7	(Damon Hill 2nd)
1995	17	7	3	7	(Damon Hill 2nd)
1996	16	5	1	8	**Damon Hill**
1997	17	4	1	2	(David Coulthard 3rd)
1998	16	4	2	2	(David Coulthard 3rd)
1999	16	4	2	6	(Eddie Irvine 2nd)
2000	17	4	1	3	(David Coulthard 3rd)
2001	17	3	1	2	(David Coulthard 2nd)
2002	17	5	1	1	(David Coulthard 4th)

*Key: * denotes a win shared with another driver.*

The Man Most Likely: David Coulthard still dreams of World title glory with McLaren.

THE TRACKS 2003

No two grand prix circuits are alike. Here are the 16 World Championship venues, with a guide to what makes each such a special arena in which our Grand Prix gladiators do battle, and a preview of the new tracks set to hold races in 2004.

Sixteen Grands Prix spread between 14 different countries (Germany and Italy host the European and San Marino Grands Prix, respectively, alongside their own) around the world make for an exceedingly international sport. Glance at a circuit map, and you may spot certain similarities in shape and length, but none are similar in the flesh, with their differences magnified by the unique atmosphere that each evokes.

Formula One fans should glory in these differences. Take Suzuka and Magny-Cours, for example, and the differences between them could not be more marked, as one

track climbs and falls on a Japanese hillside, the other undulates gently among green fields. Montreal's track is on an island, Melbourne's around a lake in a city park. At Hockenheim, the fans drink beer. At Monza, their tipple is Chianti. Then there are the climates of Sepang and Silverstone that are also poles apart, as you would expect since the former is in sub-tropical Malaysia, the latter in England.

The greatest difference of all, though, is spectators' behaviour. Interlagos and Monaco are at opposite ends of the scale of decorum, with the Brazilians chanting, dancing and waving flags with raucous

abandon while the international jet-set who assemble on the yachts in Monaco's harbour and on the balconies of the hotels and appartments above are rather more restrained, making little more noise than the chink of the ice in their gin and tonics. Another of the many attractions of the Formula One World Championship is that each and every circuit visited has a particular charm, a special historical significance or, in the case of the A1-Ring, simply a wonderful view. No one can say the World Championship has a homogenous setting.

The circuit owners themselves know that they too must be on their toes, with the World Championship's promoter Bernie Ecclestone having made it plain that he wants to drop a few European-based Grands Prix over the next few years to accommodate the introduction of races spread further around the globe.

The Belgian GP at the legendary Spa-Francorchamps has already gone, dropped last autumn after the Belgian government refused to reverse a decision to ban the cars

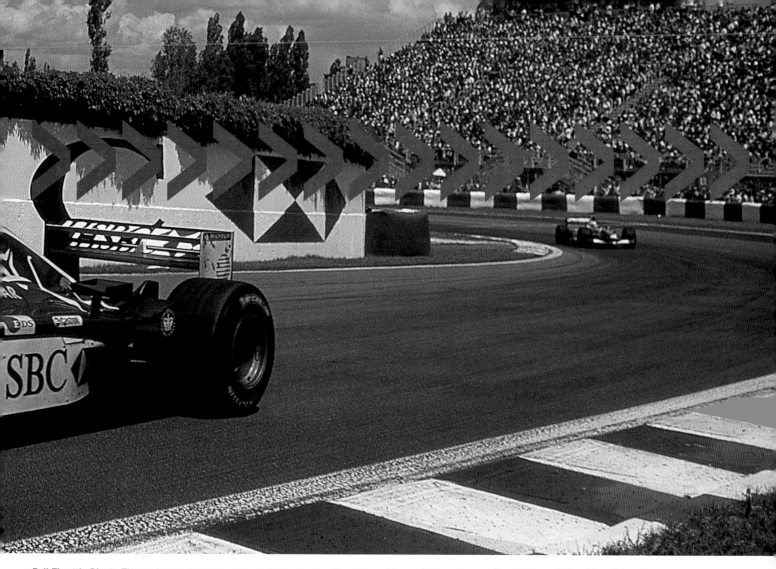

Full Throttle Blast: The tracks are changing shape, but Formula One fans the world over still love to see a Grand Prix car being driven flat-out

from running with tobacco sponsorship. And this is a massive shame.

Bahrain and China are now at the head of the queue, having signed to join the circus in 2004, with Russia and Turkey among those anxious to host a round. Indeed, with the money in place, the construction work in Bahrain started last autumn, and it announced at last September's Italian Grand Prix that it has signed a contract for a Grand Prix in 2004. The Chinese GP is planned for a new track near Shanghai. The long-awaited Russian GP, a must-have event since the fall of communism in the late 1980s, has taken a backward step, with the planned circuit on Moscow's Nagatino Island being canned. Rival city St Petersburg is working flat-out to fill the gap.

So, which Grands Prix in Europe are under threat? Silverstone, home of the British Grand Prix, topped the list following the roasting it received from Ecclestone when his helicopter was re-routed because of fog and he found the circuit's internal signposts inadequate as he battled his way in on race morning.

For now, though, the Austrian and San Marino Grands Prix appear to be the most likely for the chop. The Hungaroring has a six-year contract to host a Grand Prix, but contracts appear to count for little where big money is involved. However, the situation changes daily, so Ecclestone has let it be known that no circuit can rest on its laurels.

Every Formula One fan has a favourite circuit or a favourite Grand Prix, but change is good for all concerned, providing a refreshing new challenge for everybody, as well as a whole raft of new experiences for driver and fan alike. If you can't make it to the 16 races in 2003, enjoy the highlights and special features at each track.

A Firm Favourite: The glitz and glamour of Monaco keeps this race firmly on the calendar

Melbourne

A GREAT PLACE TO START

Located just south of the centre of Melbourne, the circuit built in rundown Albert Park for 1997 may not be a high-speed sweeper like Spa-Francorchamps or Suzuka, but it's an ample challenge for the teams and drivers as they kick off their new season.

INSIDE TRACK

DATE	9 March
CIRCUIT NAME	Albert Park
CIRCUIT LENGTH	3.295 miles/5.303km
NUMBER OF LAPS	58
LAP RECORD	Michael Schumacher (Ferrari), 1m28.214s, 134.468mph/216.396kph, 2001
TELEPHONE	00 61 3 92587100
WEBSITE	www.grandprix.com.au

PREVIOUS WINNERS

1997	David Coulthard	McLaren
1998	Mika Hakkinen	McLaren
1999	Eddie Irvine	Ferrari
2000	Michael Schumacher	Ferrari
2001	Michael Schumacher	Ferrari
2002	Michael Schumacher	Ferrari

Ambience: The Australian GP is a party in the park, embraced both by the local populace and by local business, with corporate suites packed even on the Thursday. Bars and merchandise stalls spill over the pavements in the neighbouring streets, with cheery officials adding to the well organised fun. Running a top sporting event is not a matter of chance, and Australia does it better than anyone.

Local hero: Melbourne is Alan Jones's home town, so the 1980 World Champion is always on hand.

Celebrities: The Australian GP is always packed with celebrities from film, television and sport. There's even a celebrity race, a surefire opportunity to see spins aplenty and typical 100 per cent Aussie sporting commitment.

Support acts: The Australian GP has the best package of support races of all, with the mighty V8 touring cars backed up by sportscar, Formula Ford and historic touring car races as well as sundry flypasts and parades.

Transport: Just a short ride by tram from Melbourne's city centre, Albert Park is easy to reach, with entrances alongside the stations that surround the course. There is absolutely no need to drive. Indeed, as the trackside banners tell you, don't drink too much beer then drive home as "if you drink and drive you're a bleedin' idiot"! Nicely put...

Its flat layout twists around a lake that is in the centre of the park. The circuit offers no long straights, yet, despite half a dozen tightish bends, there's still a 134mph average lap speed. Worryingly for novice drivers, any mistake is punished by the all-surrounding concrete walls.

There are large run-off areas at Turn 1, but the viewing remains excellent. The action there can be spectacular, too, as shown by Ralf Schumacher's aerial ride last year after his clash with Rubens Barrichello on the run to the first corner of the opening lap. Turn 3 offers another chance to see the cars trying to overtake as the drivers haul their cars down to low speed for this tight right. Finally, Turn 12 also sorts the men from the boys.

Now that Melbourne is established as the opening event of the World Championship calendar, any changes over the close season at Albert Park tend to be made to the spectators' environment rather than to the racing surface.

With numerous temporary grandstands backing either onto the lake or the park's golf course, the setting is very peaceful for spectators – once the engines are switched off. And, with the sea just a few blocks away behind the start/finish straight, visitors can unwind further at the end of the day.

Metropolitan Skyline: Melbourne is one of the few tracks located close to a city centre

Sepang

AN EASTERN CLASSIC

There used to be a charge levelled at circuits designed in the 1980s and 1990s that they were "Mickey Mouse". That is to say that they were not very challenging. This charge, however, can certainly not be levelled at Sepang.

Designed by the man who seems involved with every circuit change that Formula One faces, Hermann Tilke, Sepang is a gently undulating masterpiece with flowing corners that actually present drivers with the opportunity to overtake, something that has become all too rare in recent years. The key to this is that Tilke made the circuit wide, particularly at points where a long straight feeds into a tight corner, as at Turn 1, Turn 4 and Turn 15. Better still, each of these straights issues from a slow corner, enabling the attacking driver to get right into the slipstream of the car ahead.

One of the best features of the track is that the spectator banks are high, affording a good view. The main grandstand is higher still, allowing ticket holders the chance to see either all of the first half of the lap or all of the second half. Shade from the burning sun is a must, with the canopy above the main grandstand offering adequate shading.

Located 30km to the south of capital Kuala Lumpur, the track wasn't previously particularly accessible, but now it's served by a new railway link to both the city and the nearby airport.

INSIDE TRACK

DATE	23 March
CIRCUIT NAME	Sepang
CIRCUIT LENGTH	3.444 miles/5.542km
NUMBER OF LAPS	56
LAP RECORD	Montoya (Williams), 1m38.049s, 126.451mph/203.494kph, 2002
TELEPHONE	00 60 3 85262000
WEBSITE	www.malaysiangp.com.my

PREVIOUS WINNERS

1999	Eddie Irvine	Ferrari
2000	Michael Schumacher	Ferrari
2001	Michael Schumacher	Ferrari
2002	Ralf Schumacher	Williams

Sky high temperatures: The working conditions at Sepang can be quite horrendous. It's fine for the big-wigs and sponsors who can hide away in their air-conditioned suites, but out in the open, the 40-degree heat and soaring humidity really floor the mechanics.

Fluid loss: The drivers themselves have to experience purgatory, as the temperature and humidity cause them to lose many litres of body fluid during the course of the race.

Unusual visitors: The ranks of spectators are filled with many Europeans who are combining a visit to the Grand Prix with a holiday to Malaysia's beautiful islands. The numbers are also augmented by South Africans for whom this is one of the cheapest Grands Prix to visit.

Watch out for snakes: Drivers used to run the risk if they broke down at the old-shaped Hockenheim of becoming lost in the forest if they tried to walk back to the pits. A bigger risk at Sepang would be standing on a snake...

Local heroes: There are none yet, even though Malaysia's Alex Yoong tried to fill that gap in 2002. Trouble is, many Malaysians accept only winners, something that even the hard-charging Australian Mark Webber couldn't do in a Minardi last year.

Do see: Kuala Lumpur's Petronas Twin Towers and Chinese market.

Local Favourite: Alex Yoong entertained the crowd in 2002, but he won't be racing this year

Interlagos

F1'S MARDI GRAS PARTY

Attending the Brazilian Grand Prix at Interlagos is a truly heady experience, one unmatched by any other circuit on the World Championship calendar.

A challenging circuit, decaying facilities, a wild crowd and usually blazing sunshine make for a surprisingly fine mix that you won't find elsewhere.

Built on the southern edge of Sao Paulo in the early 1950s, Interlagos has long since been enveloped by this fast-expanding metropolis. But what marks it out as a great place to watch sport is that it sits wonderfully in an amphitheatre, with fabulous views from the grandstands that line the top of the hill.

Brazil's hot and wet climate leaves the playing surface bumpier than that at any other circuit visited by Formula One, making the drivers really work for their living in the heat. It's not just the bumps and the heat that tires them, though, as the dipping and squirming first corner is a real test, as is the entire twisting section from Pinheirinho to the uphill entry to the start/finish straight at Arquibancadas, with Mergulho especially testing. For overtaking opportunities, look to Descida do Lago and that first corner.

When taking in the view from the top of the circuit, the glory of the original circuit can clearly be made out as it wraps itself around the current layout, fitting almost twice the lap length into the same area. You can even see how the first corner used to be banked, running around the outside of a bowl. Wicked!

INSIDE TRACK

DATE:	6 April
CIRCUIT NAME	Interlagos
CIRCUIT LENGTH	2.667 miles/4.292km
NUMBER OF LAPS	71
LAP RECORD:	M Schumacher (Ferrari), 1m14.755s, 128.436mph/206.687kph,2000
TELEPHONE	00 55 11 813 5775
WEBSITE	www.interlagos.com

PREVIOUS WINNERS

1993	Ayrton Senna	McLaren
1994	Michael Schumacher	Benetton
1995	Michael Schumacher	Benetton
1996	Damon Hill	Williams
1997	Jacques Villeneuve	Williams
1998	Mika Hakkinen	McLaren
1999	Mika Hakkinen	McLaren
2000	Michael Schumacher	Ferrari
2001	David Coulthard	McLaren
2002	Michael Schumacher	Ferrari

Basic facilities: There's no way that even the thickest pair of rose tinted spectacles would enable the circuit's most one-eyed supporter to say that Interlagos has kept up with the times. Put simply, the facilities here are dreadful and decaying. Its paddock has been expanded in recent years, but teams still have to clamber over the packing cases in which their equipment travels to fly-away races outside Europe.

Wild crowd: At dawn on race morning, the queues stretch seemingly for ever. Then, once within the circuit's confines, the tens of thousands of Brazilians sing themselves hoarse and dance themselves stupid. If Barrichello leads the race, the volume doubles. If he retires, they slope off early.

Cooling down: When the temperatures soar, fire trucks pull up in front of the grandstands and hose down the crowd to keep them cool. Only those in the cheap seats, mind...

Pele, Pele: The greatest footballer of all time is always present, as a huge Formula One fan. Trouble was, last year, he failed to wave the chequered flag as the winning car crossed the line. Oops!

Transport tip: Take a taxi direct from your hotel and don't walk around carrying anything valuable, other than your entrance ticket.

Super Sweepers: Brazilian fans are treated with wonderful views. This is is the one from Laranja

Imola

The idea of visiting Italy in early spring is always a welcoming one, with blossom, sunshine and Chianti. However, the weather isn't always as warm or dry as one would hope. And, sadly, the circuit is now lagging behind the standards of the day.

INSIDE TRACK

DATE	20 April
CIRCUIT NAME	Imola
CIRCUIT LENGTH	3.064 miles/4.930km
NUMBER OF LAPS	62
LAP RECORD:	Barrichello (Ferrari), 1m24.170s, 131.049mph/210.893kph, 2002
TELEPHONE	00 39 0542 34116
WEBSITE	www.autodromoimola.com

PREVIOUS WINNERS

1993	Alain Prost	Williams
1994	Michael Schumacher	Benetton
1995	Damon Hill	Williams
1996	Damon Hill	Williams
1997	Heinz-Harald Frentzen	Williams
1998	David Coulthard	McLaren
1999	Michael Schumacher	Ferrari
2000	Michael Schumacher	Ferrari
2001	Ralf Schumacher	Williams
2002	Michael Schumacher	Ferrari

Tifosi country: Imola's grandstands and spectator banking is draped in red, packed with Ferrari-loving Tifosi who lap up their first chance to see the year's new Ferraris in the flesh. Unless they live close to Ferrari's Fiorano and Mugello test tracks that is...

Sad memories: Imola has claimed many a life over the years, but the dark days of 1994 still sadden, after novice Roland Ratzenberger was killed in qualifying and then multiple World Champion Ayrton Senna died the following day when he crashed out of the lead of the race.

A tight fit: The paddock is one of the smallest in Formula One, squeezed as it is between the back of the pits and the river behind.

Shaky viewpoints: A good view is much valued by the Tifosi, with rickety, home-made grandstands and tree platforms their chosen vantage points from which to watch their beloved red Ferraris in action.

Home at last: After a trio of races in Australia, Malaysia and Brazil, the teams all consider this to be their first race on home ground back in Europe, as this is the first to which they can despatch their transporters.

In memoriam: The circuit's full name is the Autodromo Enzo e Dino Ferrari in honour of the Ferrari founder's son who succumbed to a fatal illness in his 30s.

Onwards And Upwards: From Tosa, the drivers have to accelerate hard up the hill to Piratella

In truth, at a time when Bernie Ecclestone is looking to shed a European Grand Prix or two to make room for more around the globe, Imola's position looks increasingly tenuous, especially as it sits alongside another in the same country: Monza. Yes, yes, I know that Imola hosts the San Marino Grand Prix, but that kids nobody. After all, do you think it would wash if Donington Park hosted the Isle of Man Grand Prix?

Sitting pretty in a parkland setting in the north-eastern suburbs of Imola some 33km south-east of Bologna, the circuit is wonderfully undulating. Its lap starts with a series of short straights interrupted by chicanes along the bottom of the valley before heading uphill from Tosa to Piratella. A great place to watch is at the downhill Acque Minerali, or at the snappy Variante Alta. The entry of Rivazza remains a good place to look for overtaking, before the circuit takes another left and snakes back to the start/finish straight.

New for 2003, the chicane at Villeneuve is being turned into a straight, as is Variante Bassa, with the second Rivazza being made more open to encourage a faster exit speed. Variante Alta is also being modified slightly.

>> Barcelona

SOMETHING FOR EVERYONE

INSIDE TRACK

DATE	4 May
CIRCUIT NAME	Circuit de Catalunya
CIRCUIT LENGTH	2.949 miles/4.727km
NUMBER OF LAPS	65
LAP RECORD:	M Schumacher (Ferrari), 1m20.355s,132.119mph/212.615kph, 2002
TELEPHONE	00 34 93 5719771
WEBSITE	www.circuitcat.com

PREVIOUS WINNERS

1993	Alain Prost	Williams
1994	Damon Hill	Williams
1995	Michael Schumacher	Benetton
1996	Michael Schumacher	Ferrari
1997	Jacques Villeneuve	Williams
1998	Mika Hakkinen	McLaren
1999	Mika Hakkinen	McLaren
2000	Mika Hakkinen	McLaren
2001	Michael Schumacher	Ferrari
2002	Michael Schumacher	Ferrari

Over The Crest: The main straight is the longest in Formula One as it drops to the first corner

Motorbike racing is by far Spain's most popular form of motor racing, but its history of four-wheeled sport is also long and rich.

Host of a World Championship race since 1951, Spain has moved its Grand Prix around and the Circuit de Catalunya is its fifth home since then.

Located close to the village of Montmelo 20km north of Barcelona, the circuit has one of Formula One's longest straights. As this leads into a tight first corner, you'd have thought that there ought to be plenty of overtaking. However, although this is the case on the opening lap, the corner feeding onto the straight, New Holland, is fifth gear making it very difficult for a following car to stay close enough through the corner to catch a tow. The speed of the cars through New Holland makes it a great place to watch in qualifying, though, as drivers struggle to stay on the track through there. Another great viewing point is Campsa at the crest of the hill on the back section of the track. Not only does it afford a view over much of the track, but the drivers are again working hard to keep their cars on line over the brow.

Another great view is provided by the 5,000 extra seats in the main grandstand on the start/finish straight. An extra deck was built and used for the first time in 2002. This brought capacity to 10,000, with a deck of 21 hospitality boxes and 40 TV commentary suites, built at a cost of over 13 million Euros.

Party time: Melbourne has a lot to offer, Kuala Lumpur is exotic and Sao Paulo can be intimidating, but Barcelona stands out like a beacon as the first fun place for Formula One fans to go each season. The city is truly wonderful, with art, architecture and restaurants galore. Head for the Rambla.

Faded glory: Montjuich Park is but a stone's throw from the city centre, but this famous park contains more than the recent Olympic athletics stadium. Indeed, around its perimeter lies one of Europe's most fearsome Grand Prix circuits, of the same name, that enthralled fans between 1933 and 1975 when an accident that killed four spectators brought the curtains down.

Town and country: The Circuit de Catalunya is surrounded by fields and orchards as well as light industry.

Going by train: Head for Montmelo and then walk up the hill to the circuit.

Testing, testing: The circuit is one of the most used by Formula One for testing, thanks both to its mixture of fast and slow corners and its clement weather.

Famous races: There was a battle royal between Nigel Mansell and Ayrton Senna here in 1991, with the English Williams driver winning a wheel-to-wheel tussle down the straight.

A-1 Ring

FULL OF ALPINE CHARM

No circuit in the world offers a more spectacular setting than the A1-Ring. Moulded into a forested Alpine hillside overlooking a wide valley and the snow-capped mountains beyond, it's the closest that Formula One gets to nature.

No wonder it's rustic, as it's fully 70km north-west of its closest major town, Graz. Austria's second city, Salzburg, is further away, 200km to the north-west.

Those with a long memory will know that the A1-Ring sits atop one of Formula One's fabled circuits: the Osterreichring. Now one of the shortest tracks on the calendar, the A1-Ring is effectively a truncated version of the magnificent Osterreichring that hosted the Austrian GP from 1970 until 1987, with its corners tightened up and the race-winning average speed cut from 146mph to last year's 130mph.

Without the glorious Hella Licht and Bosch curves of old, the A1-Ring offers the longest climb in Formula One from the startline to the Remus Kurve which, along with the first corner, Castrol Kurve, offers one of the year's best overtaking places. Indeed, the drivers invariably tangle at the Castrol Kurve on the opening lap as they crest the brow and have to turn tight right.

The downhill stretch from the Gosser Kurve through the Niki Lauda and Power Horse Kurves is a bit "Mickey Mouse", but there's a sting in the tail at the lap-ending Jochen Rindt Kurve/A1 Kurve combo, where drivers have very little space in which to get their cars turned.

INSIDE TRACK	
DATE	18 May
CIRCUIT NAME	A1-Ring
CIRCUIT LENGTH	2.685 miles/4.326km
NUMBER OF LAPS	71
LAP RECORD:	M Schumacher (Ferrari), 1m09.298s, 139.485mph/224.468kph, 2002
TELEPHONE	00 43 3512 70930
WEBSITE	www.a1ring.at

PREVIOUS WINNERS

1984	Niki Lauda	McLaren
1985	Alain Prost	McLaren
1986	Alain Prost	McLaren
1987	Nigel Mansell	Williams
1997	Jacques Villeneuve	Williams
1998	Mika Hakkinen	McLaren
1999	Eddie Irvine	Ferrari
2000	Mika Hakkinen	McLaren
2001	David Coulthard	McLaren
2002	Michael Schumacher	Ferrari

Under local management: Not only has Austria enjoyed more than its fair share of top Formula One drivers, but two of them, three-time world champion Niki Lauda and 210-race veteran Gerhard Berger, fill top managerial positions at Jaguar and BMW respectively.

The Hills Are Alive: Well, take the hike up the steep slope to the top of the circuit and you could be forgiven for expecting Julie Andrews and the cast of *The Sound of Music* to appear at any second through the flower-filled meadows below the treeline.

Down below: At the foot of the valley beneath the A1-Ring lurks a military airfield. So what, you might think. But this goes by the name of Zeltweg. Yes, the circuit that hosted the first Austrian Grand Prix back in 1964.

Dirndls: Hard to spell, but easier to look at. The grid girls all wear the traditional Austrian dress - the Dirndl - with a lacy collar edging the low-cut front.

Mountain men: A feature of the A1-Ring is the people who appear to have come from the forests above the track down to the beer tents behind the main grandstand, wearing pointed grey felt hats and, sometimes, lederhosen. Don't worry, though, as they tend to be friendly, if seldom sober.

Riding High: The top section of the circuit is an appreciable height above the start/finish straight

Monte Carlo

F1'S MOST FAMOUS VENUE

It's an anachronism: a blast from the past. Tight, twisty and narrow, that's the setting for the Monaco Grand Prix.

A temporary track snakes around the narrow streets of Monte Carlo in the heart of the tiny principality, with its pits little more than large cupboards, the paddock an inconvenient hike away and little space for grandstands. But everyone in Formula One is prepared to put up with these shortcomings as they want to be there. Or, more to the point, their sponsors want to be there, entertaining their guests.

Bumpy and narrow, with its entire length lined by crash barriers rather than gravel traps, the track doesn't even have a proper start/finish straight, as the track in front of the pits is on a curve. The lap starts with a blast to Ste Devote, a tightening right-hander before the track climbs to Casino Square.

Then, flashing past the cafés, it dives downhill again through ultra-tight Mirabeau and the Grand Hotel Hairpin formerly known as Loews.

One of Monaco's most recognisable features is the tunnel – the fastest section of the course at 180mph – before the drivers burst onto the harbourfront. The Nouvelle Chicane is fiddly with the Tabac and Piscine tricky corners, but many find the kink before Rascasse the hardest of all.

The best news in recent years is that changes are afoot, with the whole area round Piscine set to be transformed as part of the harbour is built over and new pit garages situated there. But, sadly, this work isn't scheduled to be completed in time for this year's race.

INSIDE TRACK

DATE	1 June
CIRCUIT NAME	Monte Carlo
CIRCUIT LENGTH	2.092 miles/3.367km
NUMBER OF LAPS	78
LAP RECORD:	Barrichello (Ferrari),
	1m18.023s, 96.525mph/155.335kph
	2002
TELEPHONE	00 377 93152600
WEBSITE	www.acm.mc

PREVIOUS WINNERS

1992	Ayrton Senna	McLaren
1993	Ayrton Senna	McLaren
1994	Michael Schumacher	Benetton
1995	Michael Schumacher	Benetton
1996	Olivier Panis	Ligier
1997	Michael Schumacher	Ferrari
1998	Mika Hakkinen	McLaren
1999	Michael Schumacher	Ferrari
2000	David Coulthard	McLaren
2001	Michael Schumacher	Ferrari
2002	David Coulthard	McLaren

Celebrity heaven: Formula One has long been a magnet for celebrities, but nowhere has them clamouring to attend more than Monaco. With its yachts, casino and royal family, it has film stars and musicians vying to hog the limelight.

Massive yachts: Take a walk around the harbour and even large yachts are dwarfed by the sheer scale of some of the world's largest pleasure palaces, with many others having to stay outside on the open sea as they don't have a mooring in the inner sanctum.

Looking down on others: The fortunate have friends with apartments with balconies overlooking the circuit. The masses have to find their own vantage points, with the view down from the old town by the royal palace offering an excellent view down to Piscine, Rascasse and Virage Anthony Noghes.

No budget break: If you're heading for Monaco, bring plenty of money, as nothing is cheap. If you want to stretch your budget, stay instead in Nice or Menton and take the train in. The station is located conveniently close to the start/finish straight.

Five straight: Ayrton Senna was masterful at Monaco and won here every year from 1989 to 1993. Michael Schumacher also has a great record here too, with five wins to his name.

Down To The Sea: The circuit is particularly tight as it winds its way down towards the tunnel

Montreal

AN URBAN MYTH

Melbourne and Monaco have the racing action right in their hearts, and Montreal is the third of Formula One's urban settings.

That said, though, as the track is located on the narrow Ile de Notre Dame perched in the middle of the fast-flowing St Lawrence River, it doesn't feel that urban. Sure, you can see the skyscrapers of downtown Montreal just a mile away, but the island has a feeling of its own, open and unenclosed, buffeted by winds off the river.

Used previously as the site of the Expo '67 exhibition, the island is long and thin, with its surface area further compromised by the insertion of the rowing lake that was built for the 1976 Olympic Games. As a result, the circuit designers had little choice but to make the circuit fairly much up-and-down in design.

There isn't any change in gradient, either, to help them make things more interesting for the drivers. Effectively, it is a pair of hairpins attached on one side by a couple of straights and on the other side, the Montreal side, by a series of slow and medium-speed corners.

The Circuit Gilles Villeneuve is notorious for being a car breaker, with transmissions and brakes taking a real hammering in the race. Furthermore, with unforgiving concrete walls lining most of its length, there's extremely little room for error.

If you're thinking of attending the race and want to know where to sit for the best view, try to book a grandstand seat at the first corner: Coin Senna. Circuit modifications last year have also boosted the opportunities for overtaking into the other hairpin, the Virage du Casino.

City Backdrop: The cars are separated from the city centre by the St Lawrence

INSIDE TRACK

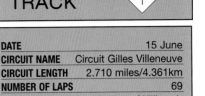

DATE	15 June
CIRCUIT NAME	Circuit Gilles Villeneuve
CIRCUIT LENGTH	2.710 miles/4.361km
NUMBER OF LAPS	69
LAP RECORD	Montoya (Williams), 1m15.960s, 128.436mph/206.688kph, 2002
TELEPHONE	001 514 350 0000
WEBSITE	www.grandprix.ca

PREVIOUS WINNERS

1993	Alain Prost	Williams
1994	Michael Schumacher	Benetton
1995	Jean Alesi	Ferrari
1996	Damon Hill	Williams
1997	Michael Schumacher	Ferrari
1998	Michael Schumacher	Ferrari
1999	Mika Hakkinen	McLaren
2000	Michael Schumacher	Ferrari
2001	Ralf Schumacher	Williams
2002	Michael Schumacher	Ferrari

Gilles forever: The circuit is named after Canada's most famous racing driver, Jacques Villeneuve's father Gilles, the winner of the first Canadian Grand Prix held here back in 1978.

Interested visitors: Drivers engaged in the Champ Car series often pop by at Grand Prix time to see friends of old who made it into Formula One, including mechanics and engineers as well as former on-track rivals.

A racing comparison: Last year was the first time in recent history that the Champ Car drivers raced on the same track as their Formula One cousins, doing so here in Montreal. The Champ Cars lapped the circuit just over 6s slower, hampered by their extra weight and inferior brakes.

Furry friends: While the A1-Ring is occasionally invaded by deer from the surrounding forest, the Circuit Gilles Villeneuve is the track most visited by our four-legged friends. In this case, the visitors are marmots, endearing little creatures – or not so little actually, as they can weigh 13.5kg – that pop up from the their burrows, seemingly oblivious to the noise.

Premature celebration: With victory in the bag in 1991, Nigel Mansell took his hand off the controls to acknowledge the crowd, stalled the Renault engine in his Williams and Benetton's Nelson Piquet passed him to win.

Nurburgring

THE TAMED MONSTER

Last year was one of change for German circuits, with both the Nurburgring and Hockenheim undergoing the surgeon's knife for major facelifts.

That surgeon was the seemingly ubiquitous circuit designer, Hermann Tilke. Reactions were mixed, but his transformation of the first few corners at the Nurburgring was deemed to be the more successful of the two jobs, especially as the tightening of the first corner provided a few more overtaking manoeuvres in the race.

The lap now starts with a new complex (Turns 1-4) known as the Mercedes Arena, with a right-hand hairpin feeding into a pair of lightly-banked left-handers and another right before descending through the sweeping Ford Kurve towards the Dunlop hairpin as before. The changes added 583m to the lap length. Climbing back up towards a high point at the RTL Kurve, the rest of the lap remained unchanged, with the section in the valley behind the paddock, from the Bit Kurve to the Veedol chicane being very fast. In terms of viewing, try the entry to the Mercedes Arena, the Veedol chicane and the last corner, Coca-Cola Kurve.

For all the plaudits for its 2002 transformation, however, any track lay-out at the Nurburgring will always be compared to the mighty Nordschleife circuit, on part of which the current circuit was built. The 14-mile long monster can be seen if you look down the hill behind the paddock.

The Nurburgring's location on a hilltop in the Eifel Mountains – 90km south-west of Cologne – means that changeable weather is always a factor, giving the tyre companies something of a dilemma when choosing which compounds to bring.

New-look Twister: Last year's introduction of the Mercedes Arena transformed the start of the lap

INSIDE TRACK	
DATE	29 June
CIRCUIT NAME	Nurburgring
CIRCUIT LENGTH	3.198 miles/5.146km
NUMBER OF LAPS	60
LAP RECORD	M Schumacher (Ferrari), 1m32.226s, 124.832mph/200.871kph, 2002
TELEPHONE	00 49 2691 923060
WEBSITE	www.nuerburgring.de

PREVIOUS WINNERS

Year	Driver	Team
1984	Alain Prost	McLaren
1985	Michele Alboreto	Ferrari
1995	Michael Schumacher	Benetton
1996	Jacques Villeneuve	Williams
1997	Jacques Villeneuve	Williams
1998	Mika Hakkinen	McLaren
1999	Johnny Herbert	Stewart
2000	Michael Schumacher	Ferrari
2001	Michael Schumacher	Ferrari
2002	Rubens Barrichello	Ferrari

Germany's other race: The Nurburgring traditionally hosts the European or sometimes the Luxembourg Grand Prix so that Germany can host two Formula One races each, along with the German Grand Prix held at Hockenheim. The only time the post-Nordschleife Nurburgring held the German Grand Prix was in 1985.

When men were men: Turn up early enough in Grand Prix week and you can pay a small fee to take your road car around the Nordschleife circuit. With 174 corners crammed into its twisting 14-mile route through the forest, it gives a clear understanding of the bravery of the racers of old. It seems incredible that it was used for a Grand Prix as recently as 1976.

Golden history: Take time out when visiting the Nurburgring to go to the circuit museum. Located on the outside of the start/finish straight, it offers an insight into the men and machinery that have raced on the various circuit configurations here since all the way back in 1927.

Tartan-chequered flag: The Nurburgring was the scene of the one and only victory enjoyed by the Stewart team – courtesy of Johnny Herbert in a rain-soaked race in 1999 – before it was transformed into today's Jaguar Racing outfit that has yet to hit the jackpot.

Magny-Cours

CHAMPAGNE SETTING

If you think Magny-Cours looks a little less than familiar this year, then that's because driver pressure has led to changes to the lay-out at Château d'Eau and at the final corner, Lycée.

INSIDE TRACK

DATE	6 July
CIRCUIT NAME	Magny-Cours
CIRCUIT LENGTH	2.641 miles/4.250km
NUMBER OF LAPS	72
LAP RECORD	Coulthard (McLaren), 1m15.045s, 126.692mph/203.882kph, 2002
TELEPHONE	00 33 3 86218000
WEBSITE	www.magny-cours.com

PREVIOUS WINNERS

1993	Alain Prost	Williams
1994	Michael Schumacher	Benetton
1995	Michael Schumacher	Benetton
1996	Damon Hill	Williams
1997	Michael Schumacher	Ferrari
1998	Michael Schumacher	Ferrari
1999	Heinz-Harald Frentzen	Jordan
2000	David Coulthard	McLaren
2001	Michael Schumacher	Ferrari
2002	Michael Schumacher	Ferrari

Middle of nowhere: To find Magny-Cours, head 250km south of Paris and 10km south of Nevers. The track is right in the middle of one of France's most rural regions, where cows seem to outnumber humans.

A rich history: With France being the first country to host a motor race, between Paris and Rouen in 1894 and a Grand Prix, at Le Mans a dozen years later, its racing history is rich and diverse.

Famous faces: Look out in the paddock, and sometimes even in the support races, for French former Grand Prix stars Jacques Laffite, René Arnoux and Jean-Pierre Jarier. Don't look for show biz celebrities, though, as the setting is too far from the bright lights for them.

Humble beginnings: Magny-Cours was a club racing venue until a massive injection of cash was approved by the then president, François Mitterand, in the late 1980s, helping it to become the home of the race.

Home number seven: The French Grand Prix is famously itinerant. It has been held at no fewer then seven circuits since 1950: Reims, Rouen-les Essarts, Clermont-Ferrand, Le Mans Bugatti, Paul Ricard, Dijon-Prenois and now Magny-Cours.

Cars from yesteryear: The circuit museum outside Château d'Eau is worth a visit, showing the track's transformation.

Slipstreaming Action: The run up to the Adelaide hairpin gives the drivers the chance of a tow

The Château d'Eau has been extended and tightened, going into more of a point. The run down the hill to the Lycée has the track kinking left before the right-hand entry to the previous chicane, then feeding into a tight right and a right-left flick onto the start/finish straight. Five-time World Champion Michael Schumacher explained why change was needed: "It was so slippery, especially when it was hot. This was not driving, it was sliding and that's for rally cars, not for Formula One."

From whatever angle its sinuous lap is examined, this super smooth track is a technical one with every sort of corner from low-speed hairpins to fast chicanes and medium-speed corners. Heinz-Harald Frentzen described it as: "one of the most exciting circuits as the corners are challenging, especially the first left-right combination."

Indeed, watching at the Estoril corner is exciting, but nothing next to the fun to be had by spectators at the Adelaide hairpin at the top of the following hill, home to 90 per cent of the overtaking manoeuvres at Magny-Cours. That, of course, is where Kimi Raikkonen lost the lead last year. However, if you really want to see the cars being worked to their limit, watch them through the Nurburgring sweepers on the drop out of Adelaide down to the 180° hairpin.

Silverstone

WHERE IT ALL BEGAN

The home of British Motorsport is fast
and open, but its future is far from certain

INSIDE TRACK

DATE	20 July
CIRCUIT NAME	Silverstone
CIRCUIT LENGTH	3.194 miles/5.140km
NUMBER OF LAPS	60
LAP RECORD	Barrichello (Ferrari), 1m23.083s, 138.397mph/222.717kph, 2002
TELEPHONE	01327 857271
WEBSITE	www.silverstone-circuit.co.uk

PREVIOUS WINNERS

1993	Alain Prost	Williams
1994	Damon Hill	Williams
1995	Johnny Herbert	Benetton
1996	Jacques Villeneuve	Williams
1997	Jacques Villeneuve	Williams
1998	Michael Schumacher	Ferrari
1999	David Coulthard	McLaren
2000	David Coulthard	McLaren
2001	Mika Hakkinen	McLaren
2002	Michael Schumacher	Ferrari

Know it alls: British racing fans are some of the most knowledgeable in the world, helped in no small part by the fact that the Grand Prix always has a host of support races, helping race-goers to spot the stars of tomorrow.

By royal appointment: There has been a royal presence at the British Grand Prix almost every year since the Queen, as Princess Elizabeth, attended that first ever round of the World Championship in 1950. HRH Prince Michael of Kent is a lifelong fan of motor racing.

In and out: Access to Silverstone has been a nightmare since the very beginning, but the opening of the Silverstone bypass last year and access off it straight into the circuit have transformed ingress and escape.

Why not stay over?: For those not wishing to tackle the traffic, camping is a popular option in the surrounding fields. Except when it rains...

Don't I know you?: The British Grand Prix is always packed with stars of stage and screen, with petrolhead Jay Kay of Jamiroquai a regular visitor.

Watch out above: Entrance by helicopter is extremely popular, with many race fans - well, the wealthy ones - parking their cars at Milton Keynes then shuttling in through the skies. Indeed, Silverstone's infield helipad becomes the busiest airport in Europe for the duration of the weekend.

Ready for blast off: Drivers prepare themselves for the race to Silverstone's first corner, Stowe

It's all down to Formula One's expansion plans, and history may yet count for nothing. The Northamptonshire track wasn't the first in the country, Brooklands was, but it has been the spiritual home since it hosted the first ever round of the Formula One World Championship in 1950. The circuit, 25km south-west of Northampton, was but two years old then, built around and along the runways of a World War Two airfield, but it has been transformed frequently since then, with changes over the past two decades removing the flowing, flat-out nature of the place irrevocably.

Nevertheless, the circuit still contains some awe-inspiring corners, starting with the first corner, Copse. Far faster than it looks, this spits the cars out through the kink at Maggotts to the bit the drivers like best: the Becketts sweepers where their cars change direction faster than seems possible. Hangar Straight is as long and fast as ever, with drivers topping 190mph before having to haul off the speed to turn into Stowe. Near the completion of the lap, the dipping and rising Bridge corner still earns respect, while the corners that follow offer great viewing from one vantage point.

A new lay-out had been due for this year, with the pitlane and paddock moved to between Club and Abbey as well as many changes to the circuit itself. However, they were shelved to work, instead, on improving the circuit's infrastructure and, after complaints last year when Bernie Ecclestone got lost on the infield, to the signposting.

Hockenheim

DON'T GET LOST IN THE WOODS

It was a jolting shock to visit Hockenheim last summer, as the home of the German Grand Prix had changed out of all recognition. But was this for the better?

Sure, the stadium section looked as it always has, with massive grandstands surrounding a tight strip of blacktop that loops around the pits and paddock. But it was the exciting section of the track that had undergone a metamorphosis.

No longer did the first corner point the track straight out onto a massive, flat-out loop through the forests. Indeed, many trees had been cleared and a short straight was now followed by a tight right-hander and then a long, arcing blast to the left up to a tight, right-hand hairpin. This in turn fed the track back towards the stadium, with a right kink, a sharp left in front of a huge new grandstand and then another right before the blast back down to the familiar right-hander

into the stadium, all the work of Hermann Tilke's pen. He chopped off more than 1.5 miles from the lap and changed forever the nature of the legendary circuit.

No longer does Hockenheim spell 220mph slipstreaming through the forests. Now, instead, those in the grandstands see the cars 67 times in the race instead of 45, with new overtaking options provided at the new second corner (Einfahrt Parabolica) and the hairpin (Spitzkehre).

As for the old forest loop, well that is being turned back into forest land, with trees planted along the old straights. But, almost as if to balance this transformation, the crowd noise in the stadium section remains as before: simply awesome.

INSIDE TRACK	
DATE	3 August
CIRCUIT NAME	Hockenheim
CIRCUIT LENGTH	2.842 miles/4.574km
NUMBER OF LAPS	67
LAP RECORD:	M Schumacher (Ferrari), 1m16.482s, 133.821mph/215.354kph, 2002
TELEPHONE	00 49 6205 95005
WEBSITE	www.hockenheimring.de

PREVIOUS WINNERS

1993	Alain Prost	Williams
1994	Gerhard Berger	Ferrari
1995	Michael Schumacher	Benetton
1996	Damon Hill	Williams
1997	Gerhard Berger	Benetton
1998	Mika Hakkinen	McLaren
1999	Eddie Irvine	Ferrari
2000	Rubens Barrichello	Ferrari
2001	Ralf Schumacher	Williams
2002	Michael Schumacher	Ferrari

Fireworks: No Grand Prix crowd is more fond of fireworks than the one packed into the stadium at Hockenheim, with pyrotechnics released into the sky whenever Michael Schumacher as much as twitches a muscle.

Ferrari fever: If the grandstands look as though they've been decked in red, that's because 80 percent of the fans are wearing "Schumi" caps. It appeared last year, however, that other drivers are starting to get a look-in.

Bam Bam: If you're looking for celebrities at the German GP, look out for the giant frame of former tennis ace Boris Becker, a real fan who never misses his home race.

Local colour: With the circuit located just 25km south of Heidelberg, many stay in this Medieval town on the banks of the River Neckar.

Hot and sticky: If you think of Germany, you may not think of soaring temperatures. However, at the end of August, it can be baking, with occasional storms building up and bursting, as in 2000 when the circuit was inundated and the tunnel beneath the start/finish straight flooded.

Days of old: Like Magny-Cours, Spa-Francorchamps and the Nurburgring, there's a circuit museum, this located immediately behind the grandstands overlooking the beginning of the start/finish straight.

Massive Grandstands: Hockenheim's stadium section buffets the drivers with a wall of sound

Hungaroring

A PASSING PROBLEM

Everyone loves to go to buzzing Budapest, the architecturally-blessed Hungarian capital on the banks of the River Danube. Yet few are as in love with the racing facility found 20km to the north-east: the Hungaroring.

Dicing For Position: The sprint to the first corner offers the best opportunity for overtaking

The circuit's setting is dramatic enough, spread across two sides of a valley, dropping down to the valley floor on the way out and on the way back again. But the problem stems from the fact that the track is both narrow and twisting, offering next to no opportunity for overtaking. Apart from the rush to the dipping first corner which is always exciting, very little passing happens except when drivers dive in for their pitstops. So, sadly, processions are the order of the day, making it a commentators' nightmare. That said, if there's a will there's a way, as Nigel Mansell proved in 1989 when he started 12th and battled his way through to

win with one of his greatest drives for Ferrari. A new hairpin at the penultimate corner may improve matters.

From the drivers' perspective, the Hungaroring is a technical circuit that keeps them busy rather than challenged, because its corners tend to be low-speed. The stretch that really makes them work for their living, and the one that can affect their lap time the most, is the section from Turn 6 to Turn 10, a seemingly never-ending sequence of esses.

From the spectators' perspective, there's excellent viewing from above the start/finish straight and also on the far side of the valley from Turn 5 to Turn 10.

INSIDE TRACK

DATE	24 August
CIRCUIT NAME	Hungaroring
CIRCUIT LENGTH	2.469 miles/3.973km
NUMBER OF LAPS	77
LAP RECORD	Hakkinen (McLaren), 1m16.723s, 115.851mph/186.435kph, 2001
TELEPHONE	00 36 2 844 1861
WEBSITE	www.hungaroring.hu

PREVIOUS WINNERS

1993	Damon Hill	Williams
1994	Michael Schumacher	Benetton
1995	Damon Hill	Williams
1996	Jacques Villeneuve	Williams
1997	Jacques Villeneuve	Williams
1998	Michael Schumacher	Ferrari
1999	Mika Hakkinen	McLaren
2000	Mika Hakkinen	McLaren
2001	Michael Schumacher	Ferrari
2002	Rubens Barrichello	Ferrari

Not so blue Danube: The River Danube wasn't its normal self last year. Indeed, it was brown at Grand Prix time, rising every day and threatening to breach its banks, swelled by the water coursing down from flooded Austria.

Finnish invasion: Mika Hakkinen may have elected to spend his summers at home in Finland, but the Finnish hordes treat the Hungarian Grand Prix as their home race, as it's their closest, albeit now coming to cheer on his successor at McLaren: Kimi Raikkonen.

Shared language: The Finns have an affinity with the Hungarians as they're the only others who can understand the national tongue. Theirs are the only two European languages that derive from the invasion of the Mongol hordes, sharing nothing with the predominant Romantic tongues.

Boiling point: The weather tends to be very hot and humid, making it even more crucial than normal that the drivers ingest a huge quantity of liquids pre-race. The fans also get jolly by doing the same, although you feel that the liquids they prescribe for themselves may not be isotonic.

Ground-breaker: The first Hungarian Grand Prix, won by Nelson Piquet for Williams in 1986, was the first race behind the old Iron Curtain that metaphorically separated Eastern Europe from the West before it was brought down.

Monza

THE PRANCING HORSE IS KING

Monza is more than the home of Italian motor racing, it's the home of the Ferrari-mad Tifosi, the most passionately fanatical Formula One fans in the world.

Big-hearted Support: There's no need to guess for which team these fans are rooting

Just one look at the red flags flying in every grandstand makes that clear, with head-to-toe Ferrari regalia reinforcing the point. Certainly they're one-eyed, shown when they spat at James Hunt as he was walking back to the pits after retiring, simply because he had challenged their beloved red cars. Mika Hakkinen came in for similar abuse two decades later. Should a Ferrari take pole or win the race, though, their adulation knows no bounds.

Used since 1922, this high-speed circuit is beautifully situated in a park on the northern outskirts of Monza, 16km north-west of Milan. The original circuit combined a road course with a banked oval but, from 1962, the steep banking was dropped for safety reasons. The decaying banking can still be seen by the first chicane.

A 150mph average speed led to the insertion of chicanes, breaking the flow before the original first corner – the Curva Grande – then halfway up to the second corner – the first of the Lesmos – and again after the downhill blast to Ascari.

New for 2002 were tall strips running across the apron inside the kerbs at these chicanes. The drivers did not like them because of their potential to damage the cars if they were run over. They had no quarrel if they crossed them intentionally, but were unhappy if they hit them avoiding other cars.

DATE	14 September
CIRCUIT NAME	Monza
CIRCUIT LENGTH	3.600 miles/5.793km
NUMBER OF LAPS	53
LAP RECORD	Barrichello (Ferrari), 1m23.657s, 154.918mph/249.305kph, 2002
TELEPHONE	00 39 39 24821
WEBSITE	www.monzanet.it

PREVIOUS WINNERS

1993	Damon Hill	Williams
1994	Damon Hill	Williams
1995	Johnny Herbert	Benetton
1996	Michael Schumacher	Ferrari
1997	David Coulthard	McLaren
1998	Michael Schumacher	Ferrari
1999	Heinz-Harald Frentzen	Jordan
2000	Michael Schumacher	Ferrari
2001	Juan Pablo Montoya	Williams
2002	Rubens Barrichello	Ferrari

Local heroes: Ferrari traditionally brings a host of its former World Champions to Monza, where they brush shoulders with other celebrities on the grid before the race. Whatever the on-track action, it remains one of the races with a real sense of occasion.

A sense of tradition: Along with Silverstone, Indianapolis and Monaco, Monza is one of only four tracks used in the first World Championship back in 1950 that's still part of the championship at the start of the 21st century now that Spa-Francorchamps has been dropped from the calendar.

Heroes in the sky: Monza's new podium impressed last year, with the first three drivers able to hover out over the pitwall so that when spraying the Champagne they can shower the fans below as well as their mechanics. For a Ferrarista to go home with clothes soaked in bubbly by a Ferrari race winner is the ultimate honour.

The ultimate spectacle: For the best viewing options, head for the first chicane, the Rettifilio Tribune, or the third chicane, the Variante Ascari. The grandstands on the outside of the Parabolica also offer plenty of overtaking potential.

Access to the gods: A tunnel under the start/finish straight allows fans into the infield and thus the chance to catch the drivers as they enter the paddock.

Indianapolis

AMERICA'S ANSWER TO MONACO

There's no racing venue more thoroughly American than the Indianapolis Motor Speedway. And none more famous.

Located in the western suburbs of Indianapolis, the circuit has drawn enormous crowds since 1909, particularly for its annual bonanza, the Indianapolis 500. Between 1950 and 1960, America's greatest race was part of the World Championship, albeit a part in which none of the regular competitors took part and from which none of the competitors entered any of the other Grands Prix. Ironically, just after it was dropped from the championship several Formula One constructors started winning the jewel in America's racing crown in the 1960s. The speed of these little, rear-engined European racers shocked the 350,000 fans packed into the massive grandstands that line all but the outside of the back straight as they'd been accustomed to huge, front-engined roadsters being the thing to have.

Indianapolis and Formula One were mutually exclusive until 2000, when circuit owner Tony George built a circuit on the massive infield, with each lap completed by a run in reverse direction onto the banking between Turns Two and One and then along most of the start/finish straight before turning back onto the level and twisting "Formula One" section.

Jacques Villeneuve – winner of the 1995 Indianapolis 500 – said famously that it had "no corner where your heartbeat goes up," but that it was a "fun track", as you have to work hard on the infield to get close to the car ahead to position yourself for an attack down the long straight.

Fans By The Thousand: The huge grandstands dwarf the enormously wide start/finish straight

INSIDE TRACK

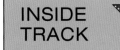

DATE	28 September
CIRCUIT NAME	Indianapolis Motor Speedway
CIRCUIT LENGTH	2.606 miles/4.195km
NUMBER OF LAPS	73
LAP RECORD	M Schumacher (Ferrari), 1:12.758s, 128.943mph/207.565kph, 2002
TELEPHONE	001 317 481 8500
WEBSITE	www.my.brickyard.com

PREVIOUS WINNERS

2000	Michael Schumacher	Ferrari
2001	Mika Hakkinen	McLaren
2002	Rubens Barrichello	Ferrari

American razzmatazz: The United States Grand Prix puts on a pre-race show that could be seen nowhere but the States, with marching bands galore, huge Stars and Stripes at every turn and every single person standing for the national anthem. It's pure Americana, a welcome slice of colour for Formula One's travelling show.

Food glorious food: There are food outlets at every turn around the huge grandstands, with the giant barbecued turkey legs a highlight, if not a delicacy.

Wonderful views: The huge grandstands afford a great view of the action, with Turn 1 the scene of the most overtaking at the end of the long start/finish straight. Turn 8 at the end of the infield straight is good too. Turn 13 offers an unusual view, as it's the only truly banked corner in Formula One.

Sports mad Indiana: Indiana's sporting heritage includes football's Indianapolis Colts, one the most exciting teams in the NFL, and the Indiana Pacers, perennial contenders on the NBA basketball court. When it comes to college teams, the most famous is the University of Notre Dame at South Bend and Indiana's high-school basketball is among America's best.

Oval racers: Great entertainment at Grand Prix time is the sprint car race on the nearby Indianapolis Raceway Park oval, its ultra-short 0.686-mile lap offering more overtaking than you can shake a stick at.

Suzuka

EASTERN SUNSET FOR SEASON

As circuit changes are made at almost every track Formula One visits, the drivers love Suzuka all the more for it is one of the few tracks remaining that really makes them work for their keep.

Suzuka separates the best drivers from the rest, with two corners standing out, namely the 'S' Curves and 130R.

Suzuka's other claim to fame is that it's the only Formula One circuit built inside an amusement park, as made clear by the giant ferris wheel and rollercoasters that can be spotted behind the grandstands down the length of the start/finish straight.

Situated just inland, some 50km south-west of Nagoya and 150km east of Osaka, Suzuka is starting to look a little long in the tooth, its paddock cramped and its facilities outdated. But the blacktop remains excellent.

The downhill approach to the double-apex first corner is followed by a gentle climb before the slope sharpens as the drivers feed their cars into the 'S' Curves, a left-right, left-right sequence where commitment and precision must be matched by a car that can hold the road. That tight sequence is followed by crossing under the latter part of the circuit then a hairpin. The drivers must maximise their exit speed out of the Spoon Curve to make the most of the long straight down to 130R, a daunting left-hander taken at 160mph. As mighty as this corner is, the final corner, the chicane called Casio Triangle, is a disappointment, but it offers plenty of overtaking potential.

DATE	12 October
CIRCUIT NAME	Suzuka
CIRCUIT LENGTH	3.641 miles/5.859km
NUMBER OF LAPS	53
LAP RECORD	R Schumacher (Williams), 1m36.944s, 135.913mph/217.728kph, 2001
TELEPHONE	00 81 593 783620
WEBSITE	www.SuzukaCircuit.co.jp

PREVIOUS WINNERS

1993	Ayrton Senna	McLaren
1994	Damon Hill	Williams
1995	Michael Schumacher	Benetton
1996	Damon Hill	Williams
1997	Michael Schumacher	Ferrari
1998	Mika Hakkinen	McLaren
1999	Mika Hakkinen	McLaren
2000	Michael Schumacher	Ferrari
2001	Michael Schumacher	Ferrari
2002	Michael Schumacher	Ferrari

School's out: There's always an end-of-term feeling in the paddock at Suzuka, as it's traditionally the final race. So it's here that the mechanics let their hair down, either by strapping one another to trolleys and soaking them or by singing in the Log Cabin karaoke bar.

Dutiful fans: The grandstands are packed dawn to dusk with tens of thousands of knowledgeable fans, no small feat in a country where perpetual traffic jams make going anywhere by road a nightmare.

Works support: Suzuka is owned by one of the motor manufacturers, Honda. And it has been so since Honda commissioned specialist circuit designer John Hugenholtz – the man who designed Zandvoort – to build a test circuit for them. That was in 1963 and Suzuka trumped the Fuji Speedway to host the Japanese Grand Prix for the first time in 1987.

Last round shoot-outs: Held as the last or penultimate round of the year, the Japanese Grand Prix has treated its crowds to some of the most famous clashes ever. Among them have been Ayrton Senna and Alain Prost in 1989 and 1990; Damon Hill versus Michael Schumacher in 1994; and Mika Hakkinen against Schumacher in 1998. It was also the scene of a livid Senna punching rookie Eddie Irvine after the race in 1993.

In For a Wild Ride: The circuit's funfair backdrop adds to the air of excitement at Suzuka

New tracks for 2004

EASTERN PROMISE

China and Bahrain will be joining the World Championship in 2004. Here's a sneak preview of the circuits they are building to welcome the Formula One circus.

It's not often that the Formula One World Championship visits a country for the first time. And it's rarer still that it visits a brand new circuit. However, it will do this not once but twice next year when Bahrain and China become part of the World Championship. As Formula One spreads its sphere of influence, new countries – with new circuits – appear on the scene. Both countries will add to the sport's international image, offering distinctly different and diverse markets. The massive population of China is as attractive to sponsors as the well-heeled one on the island kingdom of Bahrain in the Persian Gulf.

China

The sheer magnitude of the world's largest population – 1.2 billion people – is what makes the Chinese Grand Prix such an attractive proposition. After much talk of the race being awarded to the Zhuhai circuit in the south of the country – it even got as far as being on the provisional calendar for 1998 – and then perhaps on a circuit to be built outside capital Beijing, the race has gone the way of a new circuit outside the city of Shanghai. The Shanghai International Circuit will also be designed by Tilke, being built in the shape of the Chinese character "shang".

One glance at the plans reveals the hallmarks of the pen of Tilke. If you think of Sepang or, perhaps, the modifications to Hockenheim and the Nurburgring, you will get the idea. With a long back straight out of a slow corner ending with a hairpin, expect there to be at least one prime overtaking spot in the 3.39-mile (5.45-km) lap. Like Bahrain, China expects its Grand Prix to be towards the end of the season, possibly before the Japanese Grand Prix. That way, there will be more time to put the finishing touches on the circuit.

Tilke apart, there's one other common connection between both circuits: they will both permit tobacco advertising, something that few of the tracks in Europe will be permitted to do in the coming years as EU restraints begin to apply.

Feeding the 5,000: Bahrain's eight-storey VIP Centre will be able to accommodate either a number of small groups or a giant party.

Bahrain

Work was in progress on the new Bahrain Racing Circuit last year, with blasting in November proving that there's rock as well as sand in the Middle East. And rock there is, as some 500,000 cubic metres will be processed and reused during the building programme. With the full backing of the government, you can rest assured that the circuit will want for nothing. Indeed, they're harnessing the experience of the people who built the excellent Sepang circuit several years ago, building the circuit in a joint venture with the Malaysian construction company. This is even more fitting as it was the success of Sepang that spurred the Bahrainis to give the project the green light.

Ancient and modern: Blending in with the local style of architecture, Bahrain's grandstand will contain some of the 500,000 cubic metres of rock processed during the building of the track.

Right: **Will drivers get the hump?:** The provisional layout for the new track on the Arabian Gulf island of Bahrain will run close to an old camel farm.

Sited at Sakhair at the south of the island, south of capital Manama, the Hermann Tilke designed circuit – aren't they all these days! – will nestle among the sand dunes, with its lap split into two distinct parts. The first is the area around the start/finish straight, pits and paddock. This is to be made to feel as though it's an oasis, with heavily-watered grass surrounding the track. The rest of the circuit will be made to feel like a desert, which shouldn't be too difficult... It will certainly provide Formula One with a unique backdrop –

especially the old camel farmclose to the long straight before the last turn.

Formula One mechanics, in particular, will be praying that Bahrain is granted an end-of-season date, so that its arid but scorching temperatures come down below 45 degrees to closer to 30.

Bahrainis can't wait for the show to come to town, as this will, at a stroke, trump their neighbours in Dubai who have long enjoyed the upper hand in hosting high profile sporting events.

Others

Indeed, with tobacco restrictions in Europe being brought forward by more than a year, to the end of July 2005, the sport's bosses are increasingly looking for further venues outside of Europe. At the head of this list, although ironically pushing for membership of the European Union, is Turkey. A contract has already been signed for a track to be built outside Istanbul – a city astride the River Bosphorus that separates Europe from Asia Minor – to host a race in 2005.

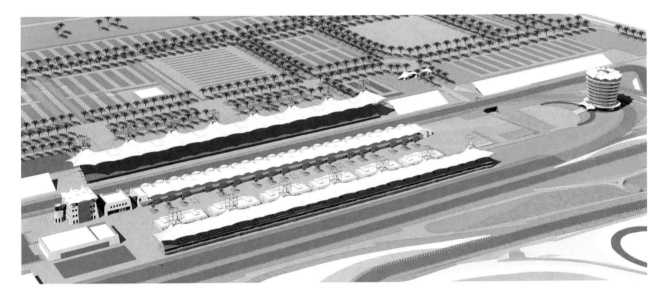

Above: **Oasis in the desert:** Bahrain's paddock and pits area will be in a lush, grassed area, but this oasis of green will become red-hot on race-days.

There has never been a season like it: Ferrari's Michael Schumacher simply dominated the 2002 FIA Formula One World Championship. Eleven wins from 17 starts was his record tally, as he landed a fifth world title to join 1950s' racer Juan Manuel Fangio atop of the all-time list.

When you consider that Michael's team-mate Rubens Barrichello picked up a further four wins for Ferrari, then the extent of the Italian team's domination is clear. The best of the rest, Williams and McLaren, won just one Grand Prix apiece, as Ferrari controlled proceedings in a way not seen since McLaren all but swept the board in 1988. There were cameo performances from a number of other teams,

but the 2002 championship was almost exclusively about the top six drivers racing for the top three teams, as only one other driver made it to the podium. But, when all is said and done, it was really about the two drivers racing for Ferrari.

You would have to have spent the past year on Mars not to have been aware of Michael Schumacher's feats. Seventeen race starts, seventeen race finishes, all on the

podium. And these finishes yielded eleven wins, five second places – some of which were the result of him letting Barrichello through to victory – and one third, resulting in a tally of 144 points. Not surprisingly, this was another record. He and Barrichello were certainly helped in no small part by a superb chassis, powered by one of the very best engines, and held to the road by the very best tyres from Bridgestone, developed specifically for their car, but some of their drives were simply mighty. Indeed, anyone who witnessed Michael's performance at his favourite circuit, Spa-Francorchamps, was watching one of the classic drives, a great champion right at the top of his game.

Established rivals McLaren and Williams were simply found wanting, especially after Ferrari moved across to its 2002 chassis at the Brazilian GP after using an uprated version of their previous chassis at the first few races. Sometimes the gap was slight, but it was always there, even though Juan Pablo

Unfulfilled Promise: Juan Pablo Montoya would often start from pole, but Michael Schumacher would drive past the Williams ace for victory.

Montoya often placed his Williams on pole position. Trouble was, his Williams tended to use up its Michelin tyres in the race rather faster than Michael and Rubens used up their Bridgestones, with the result that he failed to win a race all year. The honour of being the only drivers to topple the red duo went to Montoya's team-mate Ralf Schumacher and McLaren's David Coulthard. The Scot wasn't able to relax with this, though, as new team-mate Kimi Raikkonen outqualified him more often than not and, but for a patch of spilled oil at Magny-Cours, would have taken his maiden win.

The eight other teams barely managed to propel one of their cars into the top three. Renault, in its first year as such since taking over Benetton, ranked fourth overall, with a pair of fourth place finishes apiece for Jenson Button and Jarno Trulli, but they were a long way in arrears.

Sauber dropped back a place to rank fifth overall, with Nick Heidfeld's fourth place in Spain their best offering as rookie Felipe Massa provided the fireworks. Talking of pyrotechnics, the other most spectacular driver of 2002 was another rookie, Takuma Sato at Jordan. Both were excellent to watch, but it was Sato who elicited the loudest cheer of the year when he scored his first points, for fifth, in the final round on his home circuit, Suzuka. Giancarlo Fisichella pushed hard for little reward as the team struggled with uncompetitive Honda engines. These also slowed BAR, whose experienced drivers scored but four times all year. This dropped them behind Jaguar, whose wayward chassis wasted its strong Cosworth engine and drove Eddie Irvine to distraction. Until he scored a surprise third place in the Italian GP, that is.

Toyota stated before it arrived for its first season of Formula One that its aim was simply to qualify for races. Spending as much as the Japanese automotive giant was, their aims were clearly higher. A pair of sixths in the first three races suggested they might become midfielders, but they didn't, and both drivers were dismissed at the season's end. Scoring an equal number of points on a fraction of the budget, with fifth at the opening race in Australia, Minardi's major achievement was keeping its head above water in this most expensive of sports.

Not every team managed this, though, and one of the saddest sights of 2002 was the Arrows name hanging above an empty pit garage, something that was seen at the Hungarian GP when a delayed take-over bid meant that the team failed to show. Continuing financial problems meant that they never surfaced again, dropping the number of teams involved from eleven to ten.

AUSTRALIAN GP

STARTING WITH A BANG

Half the field was eliminated by a first corner accident and he suffered problems of his own, but through it all came Michael Schumacher to start his title defence in the best possible way, with a win.

The First of Many: Michael Schumacher acknowledges his crew as he kicks off with 10 points

The start of a new season is always a time of optimism, last-minute preparations and the release from the close-season for Formula One fans worldwide. The 2002 Australian GP was no different, but Ferrari was less frantic than other teams, as it had elected to race its 2001 car until it was sure that its 2002 challenger was 100 per cent ready.

When Rubens Barrichello and Michael Schumacher qualified on the front row, the decision looked all the more inspired, with the threat of new car unreliability hitting them in the race thus eliminated. However, Barrichello's car got no further than the first corner on the opening lap.

Ralf Schumacher made a better start from third on the grid, but the Brazilian swerved to keep him behind. They clashed, with the Williams flying high over the Ferrari. With bits flying everywhere, there was mass chaos behind, and six other cars were sidelined.

David Coulthard found himself in the lead and he edged away from Jarno Trulli, who, in

TOUGH OF THE TRACK

Not only is **Alan Jones** Australia's most recent Formula One World Champion (he won in 1980) but he's very much a local hero as he comes from Melbourne. Straight-talking in a way that is almost a national caricature, Alan was beloved by the Williams hierarchy: Frank Williams and Patrick Head. He was a man's man, a racer's racer. Indeed, so much so that he is still racing today, in touring cars and utes (pick-ups) at the age of 55. Sadly for him, Australia didn't host a World Championship race when he was racing. His father Stan won a non-championship event in 1959.

turn, held up Michael Schumacher until the Renault snapped away from him on lap eight.

The Safety Car was deployed so that Trulli's car could be moved from the middle of the track. When it withdrew at the end of lap 10, Coulthard's gearbox started changing down of its own accord and the Scot ran wide into the penultimate corner, allowing Juan Pablo Montoya and Schumacher to fight over the lead.

After a tussle or two, Schumacher took the lead and stayed there to the end, with Montoya finishing 19s behind. Kimi Raikkonen reached the podium on his McLaren debut and might have been second had he not outbraked himself at the first corner as he emerged from his second pitstop, letting Montoya back past.

With so many of the frontrunners having been sidelined, Eddie Irvine cruised around to fourth, this in a car that was in no way competitive. Behind him, Mark Webber gave Minardi a fairy-tale start by claiming fifth. As this was his Formula One debut, on home ground, you can imagine how the locals went to town. And he achieved this only by withstanding a late-race attack from Mika Salo who surprised everyone by reaching the finish for the new Toyota team.

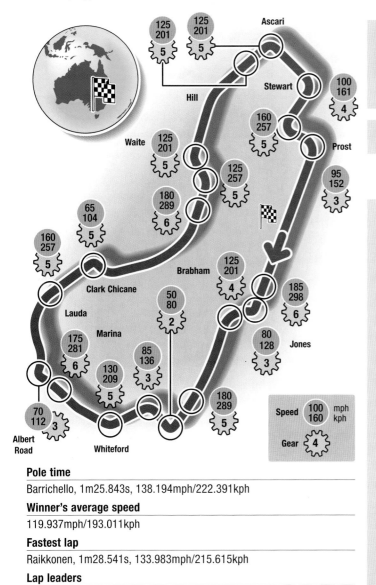

Circuit markers:
- Ascari — 125/201, 5; 125/201, 5
- Hill
- Stewart — 100/161, 4
- 160/257, 5
- Prost — 95/152, 3
- Waite — 125/201, 5
- 125/257, 5
- 180/289, 6
- 65/104, 5
- 160/257, 5
- Clark Chicane
- Lauda
- Brabham — 125/201, 4; 185/298, 6
- 50/80, 2
- 80/128, 3 — Jones
- Marina — 175/281, 6
- 85/136, 3
- 130/209, 5
- 180/289, 5
- 70/112, 3
- Albert Road
- Whiteford

| Speed | 100 mph / 160 kph |
| Gear | 4 |

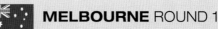

MELBOURNE ROUND 1

Date 3 March 2002 **Laps** 58 **Distance** 191.13 miles/307.53km
Weather Warm, dry and bright

RACE RESULTS

Position	Driver	Team	Result	Stops	Qualifying Time	Grid
1	**Michael Schumacher**	Ferrari	1h35m36.792s	1	1m25.848s	2
2	**Juan Pablo Montoya**	Williams	1h35m55.419s	1	1m27.249s	6
3	**Kimi Raikkonen**	McLaren	1h36m01.858s	2	1m27.161s	5
4	**Eddie Irvine**	Jaguar	57 laps	1	1m30.113s	19
5	**Mark Webber**	Minardi	56 laps	1	1m30.086s	18
6	**Mika Salo**	Toyota	56 laps	2	1m29.205s	14
7	**Alex Yoong**	Minardi	55 laps	1	1m31.504s	21
8	**Pedro de la Rosa**	Jaguar	53 laps	2	1m30.192s	20
R	**David Coulthard**	McLaren	33 laps/gearbox	0	1m26.446s	4
R	**Jacques Villeneuve**	BAR	27 laps/accident	2	1m28.657s	13
DQ	**Heinz-Harald Frentzen**	Arrows	16 laps/passed red light	1	1m29.474s	15*
DQ	**Enrique Bernoldi**	Arrows	15 laps/took spare car	1	1m29.738s	17*
R	**Takuma Sato**	Jordan	12 laps/electrics	0	1m53.351s	22
R	**Jarno Trulli**	Renault	8 laps/accident	0	1m27.710s	7
R	**Rubens Barrichello**	Ferrari	0 laps/accident	0	1m25.843s	1
R	**Ralf Schumacher**	Williams	0 laps/accident	0	1m26.279s	3
R	**Giancarlo Fisichella**	Jordan	0 laps/accident	0	1m27.869s	8
R	**Felipe Massa**	Sauber	0 laps/accident	0	1m27.972s	9
R	**Nick Heidfeld**	Sauber	0 laps/accident	0	1m28.232s	10
R	**Jenson Button**	Renault	0 laps/accident	0	1m28.361s	11
R	**Olivier Panis**	BAR	0 laps/accident	0	1m28.381s	12
R	**Allan McNish**	Toyota	0 laps/accident	0	1m29.636s	16

* Started from the rear of the grid after stalling at the start of the parade lap

Pole time
Barrichello, 1m25.843s, 138.194mph/222.391kph

Winner's average speed
119.937mph/193.011kph

Fastest lap
Raikkonen, 1m28.541s, 133.983mph/215.615kph

Lap leaders
Coulthard, 1–10; M Schumacher, 11 & 17–58; Montoya, 12–16

A Flying Start: ...But not exactly the sort that Ralf Schumacher would have wished for, as he vaults his Williams over Rubens Barrichello's Ferrari at the first corner

MALAYSIAN GP

A GIFT FOR RALF

Ralf Schumacher was delighted to come away from Malaysia with victory for Williams. However, he was assisted enormously by his team-mate Juan Pablo Montoya and his own brother Michael, who clashed at the first corner.

It was extremely close at the start at Sepang, but Montoya led the field down to the first corner, putting his nose and front wheels ahead of pole-starter Michael Schumacher. However, the Ferrari was on the inside and kept on coming, leaving it too late to change course and clattering into the Williams, spinning it around. This dropped both drivers down the order, leaving Rubens Barrichello in a comfortable lead.

Montoya and Michael fought their way back up through the field, overtaking car after car around the twists and turns of the Malaysian circuit. Montoya had to do even more passing because he was called in, somewhat inexplicably, for a drive-through penalty for his involvement in the first corner accident. Many saw this as a knee-jerk reaction following the first corner accident in the opening Grand Prix a fortnight earlier.

Out front, though, Barrichello was on a two-stop strategy and Ralf Schumacher was on a one-stopper. Ralf's speed was such that he was able to win as he pleased, and it became even easier when Barrichello's Ferrari's engine failed.

TOUGH OF THE TRACK

Malaysia doesn't have a long history of racing, with its first circuit opening only in 1968, after a brief period of races being held on temporary circuits laid out on public roads. However, it has taken rather longer to find a fast Malaysian driver. Some might say they're still looking, but at least **Alex Yoong** made it to Formula One, giving the fans someone of their own to cheer on last year, even if he was at the back of the field for Minardi. Now that they're knowledgeable of Formula One, though, the Malaysians will want to find someone to push towards the front.

With both McLarens suffering engine failures, Ralf was followed home by Montoya, albeit 40 seconds behind. David Coulthard was so upset by two failures in succession that he said that his chance of being world champion was an outside bet after just two races and that unless he won the next two races he might as well forget it...

One of the revelations of the start of the season was the speed of the Renaults, and Jenson Button came within a lap of reaching the podium, but a suspension failure forced him to slow down and this gave Michael Schumacher the opportunity to grab third place. Button kept going to finish fourth, with Sauber's Nick Heidfeld fifth.

It had looked as though Toyota would score a point for the second straight race, but confusion in the pit was caused by an unscheduled stop by Mika Salo, and Allan McNish was sent back out for his third and final stint on old tyres. The Scot duly lost ground as he struggled for grip and fell back to seventh behind Sauber newcomer Felipe Massa who thus earned his first point.

Williams One-Two: Juan Pablo Montoya joins race winner Ralf Schumacher in the podium celebrations after a race of incident

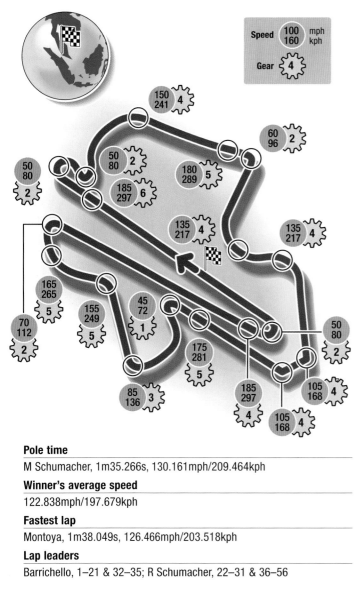

Speed 100 mph / 160 kph

Gear 4

SEPANG ROUND 2

Date 17 March 2002 **Laps** 56 **Distance** 192.89 miles/310.41km
Weather Very hot, dry and bright

RACE RESULTS

Position	Driver	Team	Result	Stops	Qualifying Time	Grid
1	Ralf Schumacher	Williams	1h34m12.912s	1	1m36.028s	4
2	Juan-Pablo Montoya	Williams	1h34m52.611s	3	1m35.497s	2
3	Michael Schumacher	Ferrari	1h35m14.706s	3	1m35.266s	1
4	Jenson Button	Renault	1h35m22.678s	1	1m37.245s	8
5	Nick Heidfeld	Sauber	55 laps	2	1m37.199s	7
6	Felipe Massa	Sauber	55 laps	2	1m38.057s	14
7	Allan McNish	Toyota	55 laps	2	1m38.959s	19
8	Jacques Villeneuve	BAR	55 laps	1	1m38.039s	13
9	Takuma Sato	Jordan	54 laps	2	1m38.141s	15
10	Pedro de la Rosa	Jaguar	54 laps	2	1m38.374s	17
11	Heinz-Harald Frentzen	Arrows	54 laps	2	1m37.919s	11
12	Mika Salo	Toyota	53 laps	4	1m37.694s	10
13	Giancarlo Fisichella	Jordan	53 laps	2	1m37.536s	9
R	Rubens Barrichello	Ferrari	39 laps/engine	2	1m35.891s	3
R	Mark Webber	Minardi	34 laps/electrical	1	1m39.454s	21
R	Eddie Irvine	Jaguar	30 laps/hydraulics	1	1m39.121s	20
R	Alex Yoong	Minardi	29 laps/gearbox	2	1m40.158s	22
R	Kimi Raikkonen	McLaren	24 laps/engine	0	1m36.468s	5
R	Enrique Bernoldi	Arrows	20 laps/fuel system	0	1m38.284s	16
R	David Coulthard	McLaren	15 laps/engine	0	1m36.477s	6
R	Olivier Panis	BAR	9 laps/clutch	0	1m38.390s	18
R	Jarno Trulli	Renault	9 laps/engine	0	1m37.920s	12

Pole time
M Schumacher, 1m35.266s, 130.161mph/209.464kph

Winner's average speed
122.838mph/197.679kph

Fastest lap
Montoya, 1m38.049s, 126.466mph/203.518kph

Lap leaders
Barrichello, 1–21 & 32–35; R Schumacher, 22–31 & 36–56

He's Inside You...: Michael Schumacher keeps on coming down the inside of Juan Pablo Montoya into the first corner as Ralf and Rubens look on with interest

>> BRAZILIAN GP

MICHAEL WINS FAMILY BATTLE

With a new ruling from the FIA hanging over them that any driver who caused an "avoidable incident" would be moved back 10 places on the grid from their qualifying position at the following race, you would have thought that the drivers would have been cautious on the run to the first corner of the Brazilian Grand Prix.

Especially a corner as tight and tricky as the sharp and blind first corner at Interlagos. But then that would have taken Michael Schumacher and Juan Pablo Montoya using the occasion to take a step back from their burgeoning battle for supremacy.

Pole-starting Montoya was ahead on the run to that opening left-hander and legitimately moved across towards the pitwall to prevent Michael Schumacher from stealing up the inside. But he didn't come all the way across, allowing Michael to keep coming. Then, when he looked ahead again, he'd left his braking too late. Washing wide, the Colombian found the German alongside him through the second part of the corner and then ahead as they rounded Curva do Sol onto the back straight. Tucking in behind, Montoya looked to make a move into Descida do Lago, but clattered into the back of the Ferrari, losing his front wing.

The lead Ferrari was untroubled, though and kept going in the lead. It soon became clear, however, that Rubens Barrichello was

Brazilian fans have a host of drivers to chose from when selecting their hero, having celebrated eight World Championships since 1972. **Rubens Barrichello** is the man of the moment, Ayrton Senna their man from the recent past, Nelson Piquet in the 1980s, while Emerson Fittipaldi set the ball rolling in 1970. Indeed, the Sao Paulista was already World Champion when he won the first World Championship Brazilian GP – at Interlagos in 1973. He moved from Lotus to McLaren and won on home ground again the following year. For Senna, winning his home race was a lengthy quest that finally ended in 1991, sending the ever-excitable crowd home delirious. Rubens is still to win at home.

Breaking Away: Michael Schumacher gets away from Ralf and the Renaults of Trulli and Button

running with a lighter fuel load. By lap 14, he sent his home crowd wild as he pulled into the lead. But, as ever with Rubens in Brazil, it wasn't to last. Just three laps later, his steaming car was abandoned.

The race wasn't over, though, as Ralf Schumacher chased his brother. But, although he caught him with 15 laps to go, he found Michael's brand new F2002 was too good for his Williams-BMW.

The McLarens of David Coulthard and Kimi Raikkonen were jumped by the Renaults at the start and then languished behind them for lap after lap. But their patience and fuel tactics paid off as they stayed out longer and moved up a position. Coulthard was rewarded with third place, while fourth went to Jenson Button after both Raikkonen and then Jarno Trulli parked up.

Montoya closed onto Button's tail in the final laps, but had to settle for fifth. The final point was claimed by Toyota for the second time in the team's first three races, with Mika Salo again the scorer.

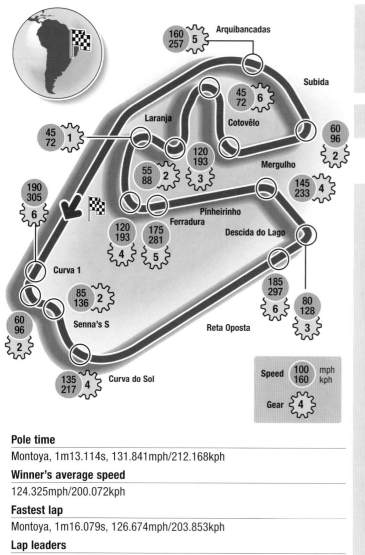

Pole time

Montoya, 1m13.114s, 131.841mph/212.168kph

Winner's average speed

124.325mph/200.072kph

Fastest lap

Montoya, 1m16.079s, 126.674mph/203.853kph

Lap leaders

M Schumacher, 1–13, 17–39 & 45–71; Barrichello, 14–16; R Schumacher, 40–44

INTERLAGOS ROUND 3

Date 31 March 2002 **Laps** 71 **Distance** 190.07 miles/305.87km
Weather Hot, dry and bright

RACE RESULTS

Position	Driver	Team	Result	Stops	Qualifying Time	Grid
1	Michael Schumacher	Ferrari	1h31m43.663s	1	1m13.241s	2
2	Ralf Schumacher	Williams	1h31m44.251s	1	1m13.328s	3
3	David Coulthard	McLaren	1h32m42.773s	1	1m13.565s	4
4	Jenson Button	Renault	1h32m50.546s	1	1m13.665s	7
5	Juan Pablo Montoya	Williams	1h32m51.226s	2	1m13.114s	1
6	Mika Salo	Toyota	70 laps	1	1m14.443s	10
7	Eddie Irvine	Jaguar	70 laps	1	1m14.537s	13
8	Pedro de la Rosa	Jaguar	70 laps	1	1m14.464s	11
9	Takuma Sato	Jordan	69 laps	1	1m15.296s	19
10	Jacques Villeneuve	BAR	68 laps/engine	2	1m14.760s	15
11	Mark Webber	Minardi	68 laps	3	1m15.340s	20
12	Kimi Raikkonen	McLaren	67 laps/wheel hub	1	1m13.595s	5
13	Alex Yoong	Minardi	67 laps	2	1m16.728s	22
R	Nick Heidfeld	Sauber	63 laps/brakes	1	1m14.233s	9
R	Jarno Trulli	Renault	61 laps/engine	1	1m13.611s	6
R	Felipe Massa	Sauber	43 laps/accident	1	1m14.533s	12
R	Allan McNish	Toyota	43 laps/spun off	2	1m14.990s	16
R	Olivier Panis	BAR	26 laps/gearbox	0	1m14.996s	17
R	Heinz-Harald Frentzen	Arrows	25 laps/track rod	0	1m15.112s	18
R	Enrique Bernoldi	Arrows	19 laps/track rod	0	1m15.355s	21
R	Rubens Barrichello	Ferrari	16 laps/hydraulics	0	1m13.935s	8
R	Giancarlo Fisichella	Jordan	6 laps/engine	0	1m14.748s	14

Oops, I missed it!: Footballing legend Pele looks at the Schumachers' disappearing cars after failing to wave the chequered flag in time at the end of the race

SAN MARINO GP

MICHAEL SENDS TIFOSI HOME HAPPY

If anyone had failed to notice at the Brazilian GP that the new Ferrari F2002 was something really rather special, there was further proof at Imola. And proof of of the fact that if the weather is less than hot, the Bridgestone tyres are superior to those provided by rivals Michelin.

Schumachers To The Fore: Fast-starting Ralf tucks in behind Michael at the first chicane

Michael Schumacher revealed that he was still sore about disappointing the tifosi on home ground in 2001 when failing to win either at Imola or Monza. Well, a last-gasp pole, demoting team-mate Rubens Barrichello, certainly delighted them. But the way that he led from start to finish sent them home ecstatic on this a historic race for Michael as he broke the record for the most race starts in a Ferrari.

Barrichello spent the first part of the race examining the rear of the Williams of fast-starting Ralf Schumacher. But this order was reversed at the first round of pitstops when Barrichello stayed out for an extra lap and then showed that he too was enjoying the

TOUGH OF THE TRACK

It comes as quite a surprise, but the hero of the ever patriotic tifosi at Imola is a Frenchman, **Patrick Tambay**. Not too surprisingly, he attained this status by dint of winning on their home turf for Ferrari. This was in 1983 when he carried the number 27 on his car, the number used until his death in 1982 by their hero Gilles Villeneuve. Patrick earned their unstinting affection for his win in Imola, the scene 12 months earlier of a bitter clash between Villeneuve and his team-mate Didier Pironi, in which Pironi had reneged on team orders and beaten Villeneuve. By winning Patrick restored his friend Villeneuve's honour.

speed of the F2002 and left Ralf in his wake, even with a slow second stop. Ralf's long face on the podium showed that he knew that the form of the F2002 was such that Williams and all other challengers had a mountain to climb to keep up with the men in red.

Juan Pablo Montoya disappointed all weekend as he failed to live up to the pre-race expectations that he would again take the battle to Michael. A handling imbalance left him to finish a lonely fourth.

Scoring points for the third race in succession, Jenson Button was extremely pleased with Renault's progress, especially as he beat David Coulthard's McLaren in a straight battle. Handling worries aside, at least the Scot finished – albeit lapped – which is more than can be said of team-mate Kimi Raikkonen who ran ahead of him until a broken exhaust was thought to be in danger of melting his suspension, so he was brought in to retire.

Of the rest, Jacques Villeneuve was again out of the points for BAR, but seventh place was a strong result as it showed that he'd outraced cars from the more favoured Sauber and Renault teams.

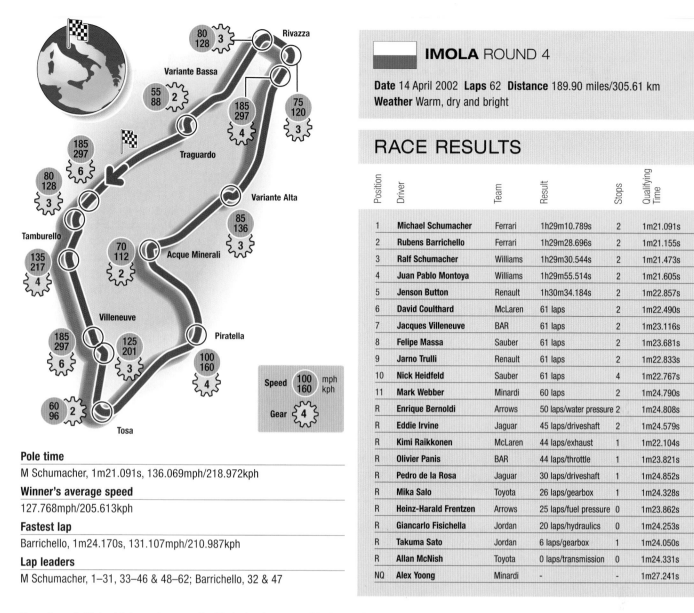

Pole time
M Schumacher, 1m21.091s, 136.069mph/218.972kph

Winner's average speed
127.768mph/205.613kph

Fastest lap
Barrichello, 1m24.170s, 131.107mph/210.987kph

Lap leaders
M Schumacher, 1–31, 33–46 & 48–62; Barrichello, 32 & 47

Circuit gear/speed markers:
- Rivazza 80/128, gear 3
- Variante Bassa 55/88, gear 2
- 185/297, gear 4
- 75/120, gear 3
- 185/297, gear 6 (Traguardo)
- 80/128, gear 3
- Tamburello 135/217, gear 4
- 70/112, gear 2 (Acque Minerali)
- 85/136, gear 3 (Variante Alta)
- Villeneuve 185/297, gear 6
- 125/201, gear 3
- 100/160, gear 4 (Piratella)
- Tosa 60/96, gear 2

| Speed | 100 / 160 | mph / kph |
| Gear | 4 | |

IMOLA ROUND 4

Date 14 April 2002 **Laps** 62 **Distance** 189.90 miles/305.61 km
Weather Warm, dry and bright

RACE RESULTS

Position	Driver	Team	Result	Stops	Qualifying Time	Grid
1	Michael Schumacher	Ferrari	1h29m10.789s	2	1m21.091s	1
2	Rubens Barrichello	Ferrari	1h29m28.696s	2	1m21.155s	2
3	Ralf Schumacher	Williams	1h29m30.544s	2	1m21.473s	3
4	Juan Pablo Montoya	Williams	1h29m55.514s	2	1m21.605s	4
5	Jenson Button	Renault	1h30m34.184s	2	1m22.857s	9
6	David Coulthard	McLaren	61 laps	2	1m22.490s	6
7	Jacques Villeneuve	BAR	61 laps	2	1m23.116s	10
8	Felipe Massa	Sauber	61 laps	2	1m23.681s	11
9	Jarno Trulli	Renault	61 laps	2	1m22.833s	8
10	Nick Heidfeld	Sauber	61 laps	4	1m22.767s	7
11	Mark Webber	Minardi	60 laps	2	1m24.790s	19
R	Enrique Bernoldi	Arrows	50 laps/water pressure	2	1m24.808s	20
R	Eddie Irvine	Jaguar	45 laps/driveshaft	2	1m24.579s	18
R	Kimi Raikkonen	McLaren	44 laps/exhaust	1	1m22.104s	5
R	Olivier Panis	BAR	44 laps/throttle	1	1m23.821s	12
R	Pedro de la Rosa	Jaguar	30 laps/driveshaft	1	1m24.852s	21
R	Mika Salo	Toyota	26 laps/gearbox	1	1m24.328s	16
R	Heinz-Harald Frentzen	Arrows	25 laps/fuel pressure	0	1m23.862s	13
R	Giancarlo Fisichella	Jordan	20 laps/hydraulics	0	1m24.253s	15
R	Takuma Sato	Jordan	6 laps/gearbox	1	1m24.050s	14
R	Allan McNish	Toyota	0 laps/transmission	0	1m24.331s	17
NQ	Alex Yoong	Minardi	-	-	1m27.241s	-

Forza Ferrari: Michael Schumacher gave the tifosi what they wanted by leading Rubens Barrichello home for a Ferrari one-two in the first of two races held in Italy

MICHAEL WINS AS HE PLEASES

Michael Schumacher had to pull out all the stops to wrest pole from team-mate Rubens Barrichello with his final run, but with the third fastest car – brother Ralf's Williams – almost a full second slower, it was clear that Rubens was the only person who could stand between him and his fourth win in the first five rounds.

TOUGH OF THE TRACK

Tough of the Track is a term that really suits the one driver who stands out above all others to be the hero of the fans at Barcelona, and that's **Nigel Mansell**. Certainly, he's not Spanish, but their own drivers have yet to shine and his drive to victory in 1991 – the first Spanish GP to be held at the Circuit de Catalunya – will long be remembered for the wheel-to-wheel tussling down the 190mph main straight between Mansell in his Williams and Ayrton Senna in his McLaren. Neither wanted to give way, but the Englishman's nerve held and he slipped past on the inside. It was a moment of pure Formula One drama.

Michael didn't have to wait long to realise that his afternoon's work was going to be conducted under minimal pressure, as Barrichello failed to get away on the parade lap, his gearbox's hydraulics having packed up.

And so it was that Barrichello retired for the fourth time in five races, joining the Minardi drivers on the sidelines, Mark Webber and Alex Yoong having been withdrawn after the warm-up in which Webber had his rear wing collapse at around 190mph on the start/finish straight. As this followed a front wing failure apiece the day before, team owner Paul Stoddart had no choice but to withdraw his cars.

Ralf Schumacher grabbed second place on the run to the first corner, making the one challenge for the lead that Michael was to experience all race. Thereafter, he settled for second, as Michael escaped by a second per lap. Ferrari was totally in control.

Then Ralf ran wide at Campsa and damaged his car's nose, necessitating a

The Biggest Smile: Michael shows his delight after making it four wins from five starts

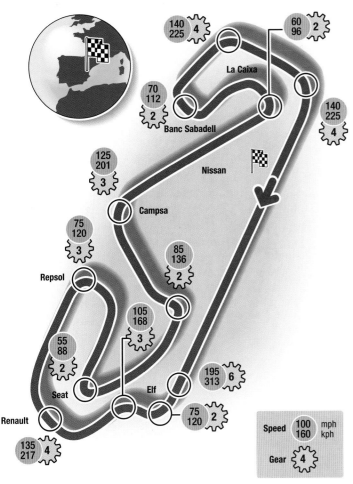

La Caixa

Banc Sabadell

Nissan

Campsa

Repsol

Seat

Renault

Elf

| Speed | 100 / 160 | mph / kph |
| Gear | 4 | |

Pole time
M Schumacher, 1m16.364s, 138.563mph/222.984kph

Winner's average speed
126.612mph/203.753kph

Fastest lap
M Schumacher, 1m20.355s, 131.680mph/211.909kph

Lap leaders
M Schumacher, 1–65

CIRCUIT DE CATALUNYA ROUND 5

Date 28 April 2002 **Laps** 65 **Distance** 190.97 miles/307.33km
Weather Warm, dry and bright

RACE RESULTS

Position	Driver	Team	Result	Stops	Qualifying Time	Grid
1	Michael Schumacher	Ferrari	1h30m29.981s	2	1m16.364s	1
2	Juan Pablo Montoya	Williams	1h31m05.610s	2	1m17.425s	4
3	David Coulthard	McLaren	1h31m12.604s	2	1m17.662s	7
4	Nick Heidfeld	Sauber	1h31m36.677s	2	1m17.851s	8
5	Felipe Massa	Sauber	1h31m48.954s	2	1m18.139s	11
6	Heinz-Harald Frentzen	Arrows	1h31m50.410s	2	1m18.121s	10
7	Jacques Villeneuve	BAR	64 laps	2	1m18.847s	15
8	Allan McNish	Toyota	64 laps	2	1m19.025s	19
9	Mika Salo	Toyota	64 laps	3	1m18.897s	17
10	Jarno Trulli	Renault	63 laps/engine	2	1m17.929s	9
11	Ralf Schumacher	Williams	63 laps/engine	3	1m17.277s	3
12	Jenson Button	Renault	60 laps/hydraulics	2	1m17.638s	6
R	Olivier Panis	BAR	43 laps/exhaust	2	1m18.472s	13
R	Eddie Irvine	Jaguar	41 laps/hydraulics	1	no time	22
R	Enrique Bernoldi	Arrows	40 laps/hydraulics	2	1m18.515s	14
R	Takuma Sato	Jordan	10 laps/spun off	0	1m19.002s	18
R	Giancarlo Fisichella	Jordan	5 laps/hydraulics	0	1m18.291s	12
R	Kimi Raikkonen	McLaren	4 laps/rear wing	0	1m17.519s	5
R	Pedro de la Rosa	Jaguar	2 laps/spun off	0	1m18.885s	16
R	Rubens Barrichello	Ferrari	0 laps/gearbox	0	1m16.690s	2
W	Mark Webber	Minardi	safety grounds	-	1m19.802s	20
W	Alex Yoong	Minardi	safety grounds	-	1m21.415s	21

change and allowing team-mate Juan Pablo Montoya into second. Kimi Raikkonen ran in fourth place, but wasn't long in the running, with his rear wing being shorn off without warning. A bit like his new "all-off" hairstyle that must have had Ron Dennis in a spin.

However, the next spin of Dennis's weekend was waiting to be told whether it was safe for David Coulthard to continue in the other McLaren. A quick consultation assessed that it was. So he did. Until the first stops, Coulthard spent time behind Jenson Button's Renault, but the Scot dived past him as the Englishman struggled with a handling problem in his second stint. Button's own team-mate Jarno Trulli then moved into fourth, but this was to come to nothing as he and Button slowed in the closing laps, dropping out of the points as Nick Heidfeld claimed fourth, not far ahead of Sauber team-mate Felipe Massa and the hard-chasing Heinz-Harald Frentzen, who scored a desperately needed point for the financially-beleaguered Arrows team.

You Can't Park There!: Mark Webber is helped out of his battered Minardi at Elf corner after its rear wing flew off at 190mph, triggering this accident

SCHUMI'S PYRRHIC VICTORY

Victory at the A1-Ring was not that held any honour for Michael Schumacher as it was one that was gifted to him by the team management at the expense of trusty number two Rubens Barrichello who'd been the man to beat all meeting.

Ferrari fans the world over would have been typically delighted with Michael Schumacher racking up the fifth win of his 2002 campaign. But it didn't look that way as even the tifosi greeted his victory with jeers and thumbs-down signals. He was deeply shocked and Formula One took a massive hit from the world's media.

Yes, the A1-Ring was the venue for the most callous piece of race manipulation seen in a long, long time, with Ferrari boss Jean Todt passing a note to Ross Brawn requesting that Rubens Barrichello – the meeting's dominant driver – pull over to let Michael through to win. Yes, let through the driver who would still extend his lead to closest rival Juan Pablo Montoya to 23 points if he held position in second. And, yes, there were still 11 races to run.

The outrage against Ferrari's tactics was immediate and strident, many saying that this was the deathknell of Formula One as a sport. In his response, Todt added fuel to the fire, suggesting that it was a business. When it all calmed down, many agreed grudgingly that team orders – even if they don't approve of them – have been used in the past to help one team driver in a title bid, but that they had no place at the one-third stage of a season. Especially not for a driver as dominant as Michael.

Understandably, the rest of the Grand Prix was overshadowed, but Montoya and Ralf Schumacher finished third and fourth for Williams, Giancarlo Fisichella got Jordan off the mark with fifth, having edged ahead of David Coulthard when the McLaren driver slid wide on oil. In addition, there was an extremely spectacular collision between Nick Heidfeld and Takuma Sato when the German driver's Sauber snapped out of control going into the tight Remus Kurve, necessitating the Japanese driver being cut from his Jordan.

By way of consolation, Barrichello had signed a two-year extension to his Ferrari contract in the lead-up to the race.

TOUGH OF THE TRACK

Austrian fans have more than their share of great drivers to choose from, ranging from Jochen Rindt – the only driver to win a World Championship title posthumously – to **Niki Lauda** to Gerhard Berger. However, it's three-time World Champion Lauda who remains the only one of this trio to have won his home Grand Prix. It was a long-time quest, though, as despite starting in Formula One in 1971, it wasn't until his penultimate season, 1984, that he won at home, at his 11th attempt. That he went on to win his third title that year, by just half a point from his McLaren team-mate Alain Prost, was the icing on the cake.

Wrong Order: Rubens, second across the line, stands atop the winner's step on the podium

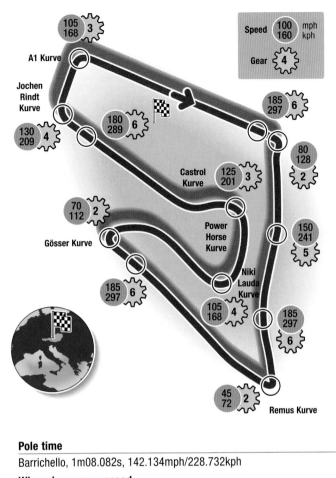

Speed 100 / 160 mph / kph
Gear 4

A1 Kurve
Jochen Rindt Kurve
105 / 168 — 3
130 / 209 — 4
180 / 289 — 6
185 / 297 — 6
125 / 201 — 3
80 / 128 — 2
70 / 112 — 2
Castrol Kurve
Gösser Kurve
Power Horse Kurve
150 / 241 — 5
185 / 297 — 6
Niki Lauda Kurve
105 / 168 — 4
185 / 297 — 6
45 / 72 — 2
Remus Kurve

A1-RING ROUND 6

Date 12 May 2002 **Laps** 71 **Distance** 190.85 miles/307.13km
Weather Warm, dry and bright

RACE RESULTS

Position	Driver	Team	Result	Stops	Qualifying Time	Grid
1	Michael Schumacher	Ferrari	1h33m51.562s	2	1m08.704s	3
2	Rubens Barrichello	Ferrari	1h33m51.744s	2	1m08.082s	1
3	Juan Pablo Montoya	Williams	1h34m09.292s	1	1m09.118s	4
4	Ralf Schumacher	Williams	1h34m10.010s	1	1m08.364s	2
5	Giancarlo Fisichella	Jordan	1h34m41.527s	1	1m09.901s	15
6	David Coulthard	McLaren	1h34m42.234s	1	1m09.335s	8
7	Jenson Button	Renault	1h34m42.791s	1	1m09.780s	13
8	Mika Salo	Toyota	1h35m00.987s	1	1m09.661s	10
9	Allan McNish	Toyota	1h35m01.281s	1	1m09.818s	14
10	Jacques Villeneuve	BAR	70 laps/engine	3	1m10.051s	17
11	Heinz-Harald Frentzen	Arrows	69 laps	1	1m09.671s	11
12	Mark Webber	Minardi	69 laps	2	1m11.388s	21
R	Jarno Trulli	Renault	44 laps/fuel pressure	1	1m09.980s	16
R	Alex Yoong	Minardi	42 laps/engine	1	1m12.336s	22
R	Eddie Irvine	Jaguar	38 laps/hydraulics	2	1m10.741s	20
R	Nick Heidfeld	Sauber	27 laps/accident	0	1m09.129s	5
R	Takuma Sato	Jordan	26 laps/accident	0	1m10.058s	18
R	Olivier Panis	BAR	22 laps/engine	0	1m09.561s	9
R	Felipe Massa	Sauber	7 laps/suspension	0	1m09.228s	7
R	Kimi Raikkonen	McLaren	5 laps/engine	0	1m09.154s	6
R	Enrique Bernoldi	Arrows	2 laps/accident	0	1m09.723s	12
R	Pedro de la Rosa	Jaguar	0 laps/throttle	0	1m10.533s	19

Pole time
Barrichello, 1m08.082s, 142.134mph/228.732kph

Winner's average speed
122.003mph/196.336kph

Fastest lap
M Schumacher, 1m09.298s, 139.641mph/224.720kph

Lap leaders
Barrichello, 1–61 & 63–70; M Schumacher, 62 & 71

The Faster Ferrari: Rubens Barrichello was in front all meeting, until told by team principal Jean Todt to pull over to let Michael Schumacher through to victory

MONACO GP

COULTHARD BREAKS THROUGH

Monaco was thought certain to be the venue for Michael Schumacher's sixth win of 2002. After all, he had won around the streets of the principality on five previous occasions and was sure to want to atone for his "gifted" win at the previous race in Austria.

Yet, when the race was over, he had been beaten fair and square. Not by Ferrari team-mate Rubens Barrichello nor by either of the Williams duo, Juan Pablo Montoya and Ralf Schumacher. No, instead by McLaren's David Coulthard, thanks both to his precise and aggressive drive and also to new, improved rubber from Michelin.

The Scot lined up on the outside of the front row, but got away like a bullet and was past pole-sitter Montoya long before the first corner, Sainte Devote. Being at the head of the field is the best place to be at narrow and twisting Monaco. And this is where Coulthard stayed, resisting huge pressure from Montoya who, in turn, had Michael Schumacher right on his heels, with Ralf Schumacher making it a foursome.

McLaren's lack of form in the season's early races suggested that Coulthard might be delaying those behind but, if anything, he was edging clear, although he was worried for a few laps by smoke coming from his Mercedes engine. This was sorted by pits-to-car telemetry and he edged further away.

TOUGH OF THE TRACK

Back in the 1960s when motor racing appeared to be the most romantic of sports, when the sun-kissed glamour was peppered with tragedy, **Graham Hill** and Monaco went together hand in hand. If it was late spring, that meant Graham would do battle around the streets of the principality, pull off his kerchief and helmet, mount the steps of the podium, be handed his trophy by Monaco's royal family then set forth for an evening of serious partying. Five times in the seven-year period between 1963 and 1969 he did that. It was clearly meant to be.

The first shuffling of the order came when Michael pitted. Then Montoya's engine blew and this left the Schumachers running second and third, with Coulthard never losing track position after his late stop. But one of Ralf's rear tyres threw a tread and he was forced to pit again. Nevertheless, he had been sufficiently far ahead of Jarno Trulli's Renault to still claim the points for third place.

Giancarlo Fisichella was in the points again for Jordan, with Heinz-Harald Frentzen able to bring his Arrow home for a second consecutive sixth place finish. He benefitted from Rubens Barrichello crashing into Kimi Raikkonen at the chicane just past the midway point of the race. The Finn retired with a shattered rear wing, while Barrichello was given a stop/go penalty for causing the accident, then a further drive-through penalty for speeding in the pitlane.

Frentzen survived a scare of his own, though, having to pit on consecutive laps as his fuel rig failed to work. It cost the Arrows driver a place to Fisichella.

The One And Only: Victory at Monaco was to prove the highpoint of David Coulthard's season

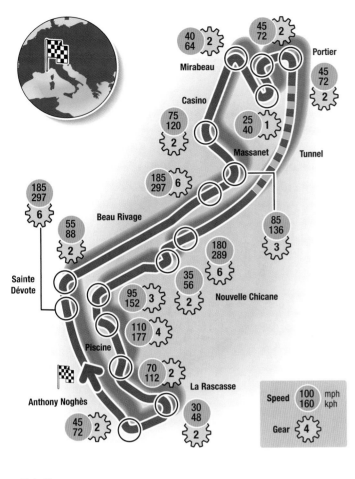

Mirabeau — 40/64 — 2
Portier — 45/72 — 2
45/72 — 2
Casino — 25/40 — 1
75/120 — 2
Massanet — Tunnel
185/297 — 6
85/136 — 3
Beau Rivage — 55/88 — 2
185/297 — 6
180/289 — 6
35/56 — 2
95/152 — 3
Nouvelle Chicane
Sainte Dévote
110/177 — 4
Piscine
70/112 — 2
La Rascasse
Anthony Noghès
45/72 — 2
30/48 — 2

Speed 100 mph / 160 kph
Gear 4

MONTE CARLO ROUND 7

Date 26 May 2002 **Laps** 78 **Distance** 163.34 miles/262.86km
Weather Warm, dry and bright

RACE RESULTS

Position	Driver	Team	Result	Stops	Qualifying Time	Grid
1	David Coulthard	McLaren	1h45m39.055s	1	1m17.068s	2
2	Michael Schumacher	Ferrari	1h45m40.104s	1	1m17.118s	3
3	Ralf Schumacher	Williams	1h46m56.504s	2	1m17.274s	4
4	Jarno Trulli	Renault	77 laps	1	1m17.710s	7
5	Giancarlo Fisichella	Jordan	77 laps	1	1m18.342s	11
6	Heinz-Harald Frentzen	Arrows	77 laps	2	1m18.607s	12
7	Rubens Barrichello	Ferrari	77 laps	3	1m17.357s	5
8	Nick Heidfeld	Sauber	76 laps	1	1m19.500s	17
9	Eddie Irvine	Jaguar	76 laps	1	1m20.139s	21
10	Pedro de la Rosa	Jaguar	76 laps	1	1m19.796s	20
11	Mark Webber	Minardi	76 laps	2	1m19.674s	19
12	Enrique Bernoldi	Arrows	76 laps	2	1m19.412s	15
R	Mika Salo	Toyota	69 laps/accident	2	1m18.234s	9
R	Felipe Massa	Sauber	63 laps/accident	2	1m19.006s	13
R	Olivier Panis	BAR	51 laps/accident	0	1m19.569s	18
R	Jenson Button	Renault	51 laps/accident	2	1m18.132s	8
R	Juan Pablo Montoya	Williams	46 laps/engine	0	1m16.676s	1
R	Jacques Villeneuve	BAR	44 laps/engine	0	1m19.252s	14
R	Kimi Raikkonen	McLaren	41 laps/crash damage	1	1m17.660s	6
R	Alex Yoong	Minardi	29 laps/suspension	0	1m21.599s	22
R	Takuma Sato	Jordan	22 laps/accident	0	1m19.461s	16
R	Allan McNish	Toyota	15 laps/accident	0	1m18.292s	10

Pole time
Montoya, 1m16.676s, 98.320mph/158.223kph

Winner's average speed
92.763mph/149.281kph

Fastest lap
Barrichello, 1m18.023s, 96.623mph/155.492kph

Lap leaders
Coulthard, 1–78

Scottish Scorcher: David Coulthard drove magnificently to lead from start to finish

>> CANADIAN GP

MICHAEL'S MONTREAL MASTERY

Six wins for Michael Schumacher from eight races was not what Formula One needed competing against football's World Cup. But there was more to the Canadian Grand Prix than that. In fact, there was action aplenty and an intriguing battle between both Ferrari drivers and Williams' Juan Pablo Montoya.

Gilles Villeneuve, who died in 1982, remains one of the most lauded Formula One drivers of all time. Sure, he won only six times and never became World Champion – although his son Jacques was, in 1997 – but it was the way that he raced that endeared him to fans the world over. Sideways everywhere in his Ferrari and never giving less than 100 per cent, racing was everything to Gilles. And this infectious approach made him popular without measure. But nowhere more so than in his homeland, Canada. That he won the first Grand Prix held in Montreal in 1978 was fitting. In fact, they then named the circuit after him, and it doesn't get much better than that.

Juan Pablo Montoya started from pole, but was chased by Rubens Barrichello who vaulted past team-mate Schumacher on the run to the first corner, suggesting that he was running with a light fuel load. He took the lead when Montoya got a little sideways at the final chicane. Michael, Kimi Raikkonen, Ralf Schumacher and David Coulthard followed in their wake, both McLarens having gained places off the grid. But soon the first three broke clear as those further back swapped places with abandon.

Barrichello then eased clear, his pace confirming his two-stop strategy. But the safety car was deployed so that Jacques Villeneuve's abandoned BAR could be removed. Immediately, Barrichello's lead of five seconds vanished, but the race changed when Montoya pitted, suggesting that he would make a late splash-and-dash. Montoya rejoined fifth, but was soon up to third when Raikkonen crossed the chicane and Ralf lost momentum behind.

Barrichello pitted from the lead on lap 26 and rejoined in sixth. This left all eyes on Michael, with Ferrari's number one giving it

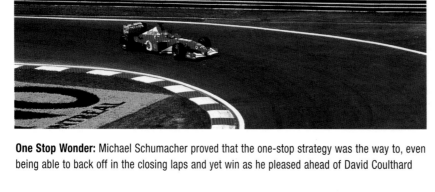

One Stop Wonder: Michael Schumacher proved that the one-stop strategy was the way to, even being able to back off in the closing laps and yet win as he pleased ahead of David Coulthard

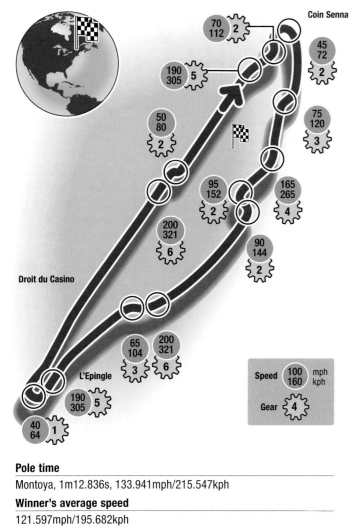

Coin Senna

70 / 112 — 2
45 / 72 — 2
190 / 305 — 5
75 / 120 — 3
50 / 80 — 2
95 / 152 — 2
165 / 265 — 4
200 / 321 — 6
90 / 144 — 2

Droit du Casino

65 / 104 — 3
200 / 321 — 6

L'Epingle

190 / 305 — 5
40 / 64 — 1

Speed 100 mph / 160 kph
Gear 4

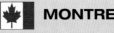

MONTREAL ROUND 8

Date 9 June 2002 **Laps** 70 **Distance** 189.69 miles/305.27km
Weather Warm, dry and bright

RACE RESULTS

Position	Driver	Team	Result	Stops	Qualifying Time	Grid
1	Michael Schumacher	Ferrari	1h33m36.111s	1	1m13.018s	2
2	David Coulthard	McLaren	1h33m37.243s	1	1m14.385s	8
3	Rubens Barrichello	Ferrari	1h33m43.193s	2	1m13.280s	3
4	Kimi Raikkonen	McLaren	1h34m13.674s	1	1m13.898s	5
5	Giancarlo Fisichella	Jordan	1h34m18.923s	1	1m14.132s	6
6	Jarno Trulli	Renault	1h34m25.059s	1	1m14.688s	10
7	Ralf Schumacher	Williams	1h34m27.629s	2	1m13.301s	4
8	Olivier Panis	BAR	69 laps	1	1m14.713s	11
9	Felipe Massa	Sauber	69 laps	2	1m14.823s	12
10	Takuma Sato	Jordan	69 laps	2	1m14.940s	15
11	Mark Webber	Minardi	69 laps	1	1m15.508s	21
12	Nick Heidfeld	Sauber	69 laps	3	1m14.139s	7
13	Heinz-Harald Frentzen	Arrows	69 laps	2	1m15.115s	19
14	Alex Yoong	Minardi	68 laps	2	1m17.347s	22
15	Jenson Button	Renault	65 laps/engine	1	1m14.854s	13
R	Juan Pablo Montoya	Williams	56 laps/engine	1	1m12.836s	1
R	Allan McNish	Toyota	45 laps/spun off	1	1m15.321s	20
R	Eddie Irvine	Jaguar	41 laps/overheating	1	1m14.882s	14
R	Mika Salo	Toyota	41 laps/brakes	3	1m15.111s	18
R	Pedro de la Rosa	Jaguar	29 laps/gearbox	1	1m15.089s	16
R	Enrique Bernoldi	Arrows	16 laps/vibration	2	1m15.102s	17
R	Jacques Villeneuve	BAR	8 laps/engine	0	1m14.564s	9

Pole time
Montoya, 1m12.836s, 133.941mph/215.547kph

Winner's average speed
121.597mph/195.682kph

Fastest lap
Montoya, 1m15.960s, 128.432mph/206.682kph

Lap leaders
Barrichello, 1–25; M Schumacher, 26–37, 51–70; Montoya, 38–50

everything to attempt to make his one-stop strategy work as Montoya piled on the pressure in the final third of the race. Any doubts about the result were erased when the Colombian's BMW engine failed and Michael was left to win as he pleased.

Second place went to Coulthard – up from eighth – was the last driver to pit and was helped by Ferrari delaying Barrichello on his second stop to clear debris from his sidepods. Barrichello emerged just behind Coulthard, even though he did edge ahead approaching the chicane after Coulthard lost momentum as they lapped Takuma Sato, but Coulthard braked later than late and went back ahead.

Had Barrichello not also run on the wrong side of the kerbing, then Coulthard would have had to let him back past. But the Brazilian also ran off line and so the matter was settled in the Scot's favour.

Fourth went to Raikkonen who had to slow as his fuel rig hadn't delivered enough fuel. Fortunately for him, Ralf's car had to stop an extra time after his rig packed up, dropping him from the points. Jordan picked up two points from Fisichella's fifth place, while the top six was completed by Jarno Trulli in a Renault.

The Big Three: Ferrari, McLaren and Williams continued to be the teams setting the pace in Formula One in 2002, again keeping the drivers from the other eight teams off the podium. It was to stay this way all season

EUROPEAN GP

FERRARI GET THE RUBBER RIGHT

Tyres were the key to the European GP, as Williams discovered to their cost. In order to take the fight to Ferrari in qualifying, they fitted Michelin's soft rubber to Juan Pablo Montoya's FW24, with Ralf Schumacher opting for the harder tyre.

Reverse One-Two: It was Michael Schumacher's turn to follow Rubens Barrichello across the line

Ralf Schumacher looked to be set for pole. Then, although out of sorts through much of practice, Juan Pablo Montoya pieced together a great lap to secure his third pole in a row. The race, though, would prove that Ferrari's Bridgestones were the tyres to have.

It's not just that Michael Schumacher had tyres that performed better in race conditions, they could have helped him to take pole too, had he firstly not had to swap to his spare car, then attacked the chicane and final corner too hard with the fastest qualifying lap almost assured. From third on the grid, Michael demoted both Ralf and Montoya within three laps. However, Rubens Barrichello was already at the head of the field after an opening lap that saw him leap from fourth place to first as the Williamses touched at the new, tighter first corner.

Both Ferraris were running with light fuel loads, aiming for a two-stop strategy as they escaped by two seconds per lap. They were on another planet. The McLarens may have been slower in qualifying, but they used their Michelins better in the race, with David Coulthard all over the back of Montoya. With their lone pit stops looming, David got a run on Montoya into the first corner. Going around the outside at this new hairpin, he was hit when Montoya lost grip and spun, wrecking the McLaren's front suspension. Kimi Raikkonen then closed in on Ralf and claimed third when Ralf pitted earlier than planned as he too had run out of rear grip.

The course of the race was sorted when Schumacher spun, delaying him by 10 seconds as he closed in on Barrichello on lap 23 of the 60-lap race. With Barrichello still ahead after their second stops, and their margin over third-placed Raikkonen truly enormous, it appeared that the order was given for the pair to stop racing as they backed off by several seconds per lap.

With an FIA hearing looming, perhaps Ferrari didn't dare to repeat their position reversal of Austria. And so Barrichello finally landed his second Formula One win.

Raikkonen held on to third from Ralf, with Jenson Button dropping behind the Williams when he came in for his second stop. Felipe Massa claimed the final point ahead of his Sauber team-mate Nick Heidfeld, who was himself fighting to keep Jarno Trulli behind.

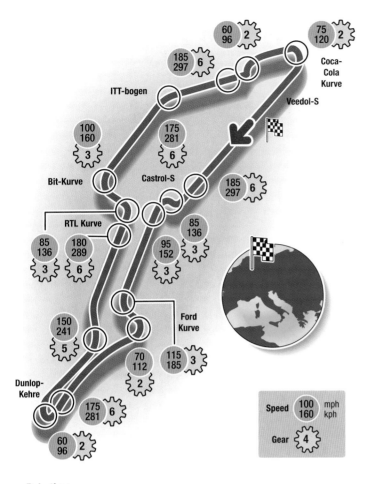

ITT-bogen
60
96 2
185
297 6
75
120 2
Coca-Cola Kurve
Veedol-S
100
160 3
175
281 6
185
297 6
Bit-Kurve
Castrol-S
RTL Kurve
85
136 3
180
289 6
95
152 3
85
136 3
Ford Kurve
150
241 5
70
112 2
115
185 3
Dunlop-Kehre
175
281 6
60
96 2

Speed 100/160 mph/kph
Gear 4

Pole time
Montoya, 1m29.906s, 128.043mph/206.056kph

Winner's average speed
121.012mph/194.741kph

Fastest lap
M Schumacher, 1m32.226s, 124.821mph/200.871kph

Lap leaders
Barrichello, 1–60

NURBURGRING ROUND 9

Date 23 June 2002 **Laps** 60 **Distance** 191.85 miles/308.738km
Weather Warm, dry and bright

RACE RESULTS

Position	Driver	Team	Result	Stops	Qualifying Time	Grid
1	Rubens Barrichello	Ferrari	1h35m07.426s	2	1m30.387s	4
2	Michael Schumacher	Ferrari	1h35m07.720s	2	1m30.035s	3
3	Kimi Raikkonen	McLaren	1h35m53.861s	1	1m30.591s	6
4	Ralf Schumacher	Williams	1m36m14.389s	1	1m29.915s	2
5	Jenson Button	Renault	1h36m24.370s	2	1m31.136s	8
6	Felipe Massa	Sauber	59 laps	1	1m31.733s	11
7	Nick Heidfeld	Sauber	59 laps	1	1m31.211s	9
8	Jarno Trulli	Renault	59 laps	2	1m30.927s	7
9	Olivier Panis	BAR	59 laps	1	1m31.906s	12
10	Enrique Bernoldi	Arrows	59 laps	2	1m33.360s	21
11	Pedro de la Rosa	Jaguar	59 laps	1	1m32.281s	16
12	Jacques Villeneuve	BAR	59 laps	2	1m32.968s	19
13	Heinz-Harald Frentzen	Arrows	59 laps	2	1m32.144s	15
14	Allan McNish	Toyota	59 laps	2	1m31.941s	13
15	Mark Webber	Minardi	58 laps	2	1m32.996s	20
16	Takuma Sato	Jordan	58 laps	2	1m31.999s	14
R	Mika Salo	Toyota	51 laps/gearbox	2	1m31.389s	10
R	Alex Yoong	Minardi	48 laps/hydraulics	3	1m34.251s	22
R	Eddie Irvine	Jaguar	41 laps/hydraulics	2	1m32.510s	17
R	Juan Pablo Montoya	Williams	27 laps/accident	0	1m29.906s	1
R	David Coulthard	McLaren	27 laps/accident	0	1m30.550s	5
R	Giancarlo Fisichella	Jordan	26 laps/steering	0	1m32.591s	18

Glory, Glory, Glory: Rubens Barrichello lets rip after racing to his first win of 2002

>> BRITISH GP

SEVEN OUT OF TEN FOR MICHAEL

Rain always spices up a race, but the result was pretty much the same as all the other races in 2002, as Michael Schumacher won his seventh race of this campaign, leaving him poised to claim a record-equalling fifth world title.

Victory to Michael Schumacher. There was little surprise at that, but the early running from pole position was made by Williams ace Juan Pablo Montoya. That was until the rain set in. Once the track was wet, unless you had Bridgestone tyres, you were going nowhere. And, of course, Ferrari wear Bridgestones.

The key was that while the Michelin runners opted for wets, Ferrari sent their drivers back out on Bridgestone's effective intermediates thanks to a snap decision by

Ferrari Technical Director Ross Brawn. So Michael pulled away at a rate of two seconds per lap faster than the chasing pack.

Michael was followed home by teammate Rubens Barrichello. Again, this wasn't unusual, except that the Brazilian's drive proved the dominance of the Ferrari/Bridgestone combination as the Brazilian driver was left standing with his engine dead at the start of the formation lap and had to start from the tail of the field. Such was his progress that Rubens was up to second

within 19 laps. On the lap following his second pitstop, though, Montoya got the jump on him out of Bridge and stayed ahead for several laps on the drying track before dropping back into third at Copse.

Montoya was able to hold onto third, his the only car on Michelin tyres in the top six. McLaren's drivers were unable to take advantage as Kimi Raikkonen pitted without telling the team and they weren't ready. David Coulthard, on the other hand, asked to pit, but the crew misheard him and he lost time doing another lap in the deluge. He later ran off the track four times.

BAR left Silverstone in a good mood. The first nine rounds had yielded not one point, but they came away with five, with both drivers having scored, Jacques Villeneuve in fourth and Olivier Panis in fifth. The final point went to Nick Heidfeld for Sauber, just ahead of Jordan's Giancarlo Fisichella.

One of the talking points of the weekend was that Arrows very nearly didn't make it to the grid. Indeed, until an outstanding bill was paid to Cosworth, their cars were without engines and missed all running on Friday. Then Heinz-Harald Frentzen's engine expired when he was running seventh mid-race.

Mighty Michael: Schumacher the elder was king of mixed weather and track conditions as he raced to his seventh win of the season

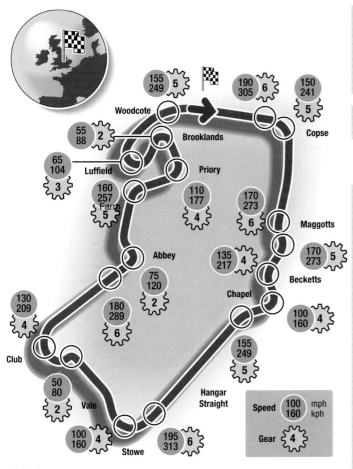

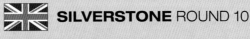
Circuit corners: Woodcote 155/249 gear 5 · 190/305 gear 6 · Copse 150/241 gear 5 · Brooklands 55/88 gear 2 · Luffield 65/104 gear 3 · Priory · 160/257 Farm gear 5 · 110/177 gear 4 · 170/273 gear 6 · Maggotts · Abbey · 135/217 gear 4 · 170/273 gear 5 · Becketts · 75/120 gear 2 · Chapel · 100/160 gear 4 · 130/209 gear 4 · 180/289 gear 6 · 155/249 gear 5 · Club · Hangar Straight · 50/80 gear 2 · Vale · 100/160 gear 4 · 195/313 gear 6 · Stowe · Speed 100/160 mph/kph · Gear 4

RACE RESULTS

Position	Driver	Team	Result	Stops	Qualifying Time	Grid
1	Michael Schumacher	Ferrari	1h31m45.015s	3	1m19.042s	3
2	Rubens Barrichello	Ferrari	1h31m59.593s	3	1m19.032s	2
3	Juan Pablo Montoya	Williams	1h32m16.676s	2	1m18.998s	1
4	Jacques Villeneuve	BAR	59 laps	2	1m21.130s	9
5	Olivier Panis	BAR	59 laps	2	1m21.274s	13
6	Nick Heidfeld	Sauber	59 laps	2	1m21.187s	10
7	Giancarlo Fisichella	Jordan	59 laps	2	1m21.636s	17
8	Ralf Schumacher	Williams	59 laps	3	1m19.329s	4
9	Felipe Massa	Sauber	59 laps	3	1m21.191s	11
10	David Coulthard	McLaren	58 laps	4	1m20.315s	6
11	Pedro de la Rosa	Jaguar	58 laps	3	1m23.422s	21
12	Jenson Button	Renault	54 laps/suspension	4	1m21.247s	12
R	Takuma Sato	Jordan	50 laps/engine	2	1m21.337s	14
R	Kimi Raikkonen	McLaren	44 laps/engine	4	1m20.133s	5
R	Jarno Trulli	Renault	29 laps/electrics	3	1m20.516s	7
R	Enrique Bernoldi	Arrows	23 laps/transmission	3	1m21.780s	18
R	Eddie Irvine	Jaguar	23 laps/spun off	1	1m21.851s	19
R	Heinz-Harald Frentzen	Arrows	20 laps/engine	1	1m21.416s	16
R	Mika Salo	Toyota	25 laps/transmission	1	1m20.995s	8
R	Mark Webber	Minardi	9 laps/spun off	0	1m22.281s	20
R	Allan McNish	Toyota	0 laps/clutch	0	1m21.382s	15
NQ	Alex Yoong	Minardi	-	-	1m24.785s	-

Pole time
Montoya, 1m18.998s, 145.462mph/234.088kph

Winner's average speed
126.330mph/203.299kph

Fastest lap
Barrichello, 1m23.083s, 138.310mph/222.578kph

Lap leaders
Montoya, 1–15, M Schumacher, 16-60

Everything Is A Blur: ...But Michael Schumacher's focus was as perfect as ever

FRENCH GP

>>

MICHAEL CLINCHES IN ROUND 11

It was always going to be a matter of when rather than if Michael Schumacher became World Champion for the fifth time. But not even Michael himself expected to do it as early as the French GP and it was only in the closing laps that he took the lead needed to do so.

Clap Hands: Michael Schumacher applauds himself for becoming champion for a fifth time

All it took to change the second place – which would have delayed Michael's crowning until the German GP – into a win was a patch of oil from Allan McNish's blown Toyota which was found by race leader Kimi Raikkonen with five laps to go. The Finn's McLaren slid on into the Adelaide hairpin and duly ran wide.

A yellow flag was shown as the Toyota was stationary just off the track at the apex, and through came the Ferrari, forcing Raikkonen back off the track as he tried to rejoin at the exit of the hairpin. So, Michael was in front, Kimi was cursing not having seen the oil, and McLaren was e-mailing race control for clarification on whether

Michael had overtaken under a yellow flag. After hours of deliberation, it was decided that he had not and so Ferrari's party was able to begin.

Michael himself had reason to feel aggrieved, as he'd been leading when called in for a drive-through penalty for crossing the white line at the pit exit. This brought him back into the grips of the McLarens, but any chance of a three-way battle to the finish was scotched by David Coulthard committing a similar error. The Scot was able to rejoin and finish third despite an engine problem.

On pole for the fifth race in succession, Juan Pablo Montoya and team-mate Ralf Schumacher opted for the harder Michelin compound but struggled for grip. Montoya led a queue of cars until his first pitstop but slipped back to an eventual fourth, just ahead of Ralf.

Jenson Button had reason not to enjoy the French GP, as it was revealed on the Saturday that he was being discarded by Renault for 2003 to make way for Fernando Alonso. However, he moved up to sixth when Rubens Barrichello retired after his Ferrari failed to fire up as required for the formation lap, and then stayed there until flagfall, putting team-mate Jarno Trulli in the shade, as if to prove a point.

Barrichello wasn't the only driver to have a bad meeting, as Giancarlo Fisichella was unable even to start qualifying, after crashing at 170mph. He was more than a little dizzy and had a stiff neck.

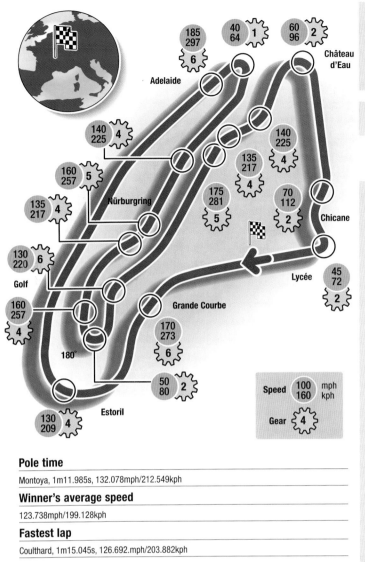

Adelaide
Château d'Eau
185 / 297 — 6
40 / 64 — 1
60 / 96 — 2
140 / 225 — 4
140 / 225 — 4
160 / 257 — 5
135 / 217 — 4
Nürburgring
135 / 217 — 4
175 / 281 — 5
70 / 112 — 2
Chicane
130 / 220 — 6
Golf
160 / 257 — 4
Grande Courbe
170 / 273 — 6
Lycée
45 / 72 — 2
180°
50 / 80 — 2
Estoril
130 / 209 — 4

Speed 100 / 160 mph/kph
Gear 4

MAGNY-COURS ROUND 11

Date 21 July 2002 **Laps** 72 **Distance** 190.07 miles/305.87km
Weather Hot, dry and bright

RACE RESULTS

Position	Driver	Team	Result	Stops	Qualifying Time	Grid
1	Michael Schumacher	Ferrari	1h32m09.837s	3	1m12.008s	2
2	Kimi Raikkonen	McLaren	1h32m10.941s	2	1m12.244s	4
3	David Coulthard	McLaren	1h32m41.812s	2	1m12.498s	6
4	Juan Pablo Montoya	Williams	1h32m50.512s	2	1m11.985s	1
5	Ralf Schumacher	Williams	1h32m51.609s	3	1m12.424s	5
6	Jenson Button	Renault	71 laps	3	1m12.761s	7
7	Nick Heidfeld	Sauber	71 laps	3	1m13.370s	10
8	Mark Webber	Minardi	71 laps	3	1m14.800s	18
9	Pedro de la Rosa	Jaguar	70 laps	3	1m13.656s	15
10	Alex Yoong	Minardi	68 laps	2	1m16.798s	19
11	Allan McNish	Toyota	65 laps/engine	2	1m13.949s	17
R	Eddie Irvine	Jaguar	52 laps/rear wing	2	1m13.188s	9
R	Jarno Trulli	Renault	49 laps/engine	2	1m13.030s	8
R	Felipe Massa	Sauber	48 laps/transmission	3	1m13.501s	12
R	Mika Salo	Toyota	48 laps/engine	2	1m13.837s	16
R	Jacques Villeneuve	BAR	35 laps/engine	1	1m13.506s	13
R	Olivier Panis	BAR	29 laps/crash damage	2	1m13.457s	11
R	Takuma Sato	Jordan	23 laps/spun off	0	1m13.542s	14
R	Rubens Barrichello	Ferrari	0 laps/electrics	0	1m12.197s	3
NQ	Heinz-Harald Frentzen	Arrows	-	-	1m18.497s	-
NQ	Enrique Bernoldi	Arrows	-	-	1m19.843s	-
W	Giancarlo Fisichella	Jordan	-/neck injury	-	no time	-

Pole time
Montoya, 1m11.985s, 132.078mph/212.549kph

Winner's average speed
123.738mph/199.128kph

Fastest lap
Coulthard, 1m15.045s, 126.692.mph/203.882kph

Lap leaders
Montoya, 1–23 & 36–42; M Schumacher, 24–25, 29–35 & 68–72; Raikkonen, 26, 43–49 & 55–67; Coulthard, 27–28 & 50–54

On The Sidelines: Arrows gave Enrique Bernoldi next to no chance of qualifying

GERMAN GP

MICHAEL COMPLETES FERRARI SET

He arrived as World Champion for the fifth time, but Michael Schumacher's post-race celebrations were even more ecstatic than they had been at Magny-Cours as they were in front of his raucous home crowd.

Amazingly, Michael Schumacher had won the German GP only once before, back in 1995 for Benetton. After pipping brother Ralf for pole – his first at Hockenheim – the newly-crowned World Champion was even more desperate to add a ninth win to his tally, as this was the only current Grand Prix circuit on which he had not won for the Italian team.

With temperatures soaring and Bridgestone-shod cars filling the first six places in the warm-up, it looked as though the Ferraris would have the legs on leading Michelin teams, Williams and McLaren. And, with a great start made to look better still – Ralf was a little stymied in his run to the first corner – Michael was safe from attacks by Ralf or Rubens Barrichello into the tight new second corner that opened the circuit's all-new back section.

As they tussled and Juan Pablo Montoya fell to fifth behind McLaren's Kimi Raikkonen, Michael was even further clear by the new hairpin, safe from attack from behind. Michael pushed very hard in the opening laps before his escape was trimmed by Ralf's rubber coming into its own.

Ralf took the lead only when Michael made his two stops, but it was not to be a family one-two because Ralf had to make a late pitstop as his engine temperatures were soaring. He wasn't the only one delayed; Barrichello had a terribly slow second pitstop so Montoya scooped second place, his best result since the Spanish GP. This result hadn't looked likely in the early laps as the Colombian struggled to pass Raikkonen who was clearly delaying him. The Finn wasn't to score, though, a blow-out costing him time as he struggled back to the pits. He later spun off.

So David Coulthard finished fifth, with Nick Heidfeld claiming the final point for Sauber, benefitting from the failure of Olivier Panis, Jarno Trulli and Giancarlo Fisichella,

TOUGH OF THE TRACK

Gerhard Berger scored one of the most improbable wins at Hockenheim in 1997. The Austrian had won here in 1994, for Ferrari, but his winning drive for Benetton came in the face of adversity, for he was making a comeback after sinus problems had kept him out for three races. On top of that, his father had just died in a plane crash. Still, he silenced his critics, especially boss Flavio Briatore, by putting his car on pole. That he went on to win made it a very special result. It was to be Gerhard's final win.

who had all qualified ahead of him.

Showing marked progress were the Honda-powered cars of Jordan and BAR, both helped by running on the more effective Bridgestone rubber, with Fisichella bouncing back from the neck injury he sustained at Magny-Cours to qualify his Jordan sixth fastest and BAR's Panis next up in seventh on the grid. Neither was rewarded in the race, although Jordan's Takuma Sato scored his best result: eighth.

Bird's Eye View: The Schumachers lead away ahead of their team-mates Barrichello and Montoya at the start of the first race on the new layout

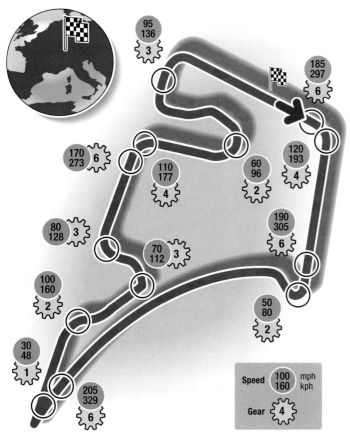

Circuit speed/gear indicators:
- 95 / 136 — gear 3
- 185 / 297 — gear 6
- 170 / 273 — gear 6
- 110 / 177 — gear 4
- 60 / 96 — gear 2
- 120 / 193 — gear 4
- 80 / 128 — gear 3
- 70 / 112 — gear 3
- 190 / 305 — gear 6
- 100 / 160 — gear 2
- 50 / 80 — gear 2
- 30 / 48 — gear 1
- 205 / 329 — gear 6

Speed: 100 mph / 160 kph
Gear: 4

HOCKENHEIM ROUND 12

Date 28 July 2002 **Laps** 67 **Distance** 190.43 miles/306.46km
Weather Hot, dry and bright

RACE RESULTS

Position	Driver	Team	Result	Stops	Qualifying Time	Grid
1	Michael Schumacher	Ferrari	1h27m52.078s	2	1m14.389s	1
2	Juan Pablo Montoya	Williams	1h28m02.581s	2	1m15.108s	4
3	Ralf Schumacher	Williams	1h28m06.544s	3	1m14.570s	2
4	Rubens Barrichello	Ferrari	1h28m15.273s	2	1m14.693s	3
5	David Coulthard	McLaren	66 laps	2	1m15.909s	9
6	Nick Heidfeld	Sauber	66 laps	2	1m15.990s	10
7	Felipe Massa	Sauber	66 laps	2	1m16.351s	14
8	Takuma Sato	Jordan	66 laps	2	1m16.072s	12
9	Mika Salo	Toyota	66 laps	2	1m16.685s	19
R	Giancarlo Fisichella	Jordan	59 laps/engine	2	1m15.690s	6
R	Kimi Raikkonen	McLaren	59 laps/spun off	2	1m15.639s	5
R	Eddie Irvine	Jaguar	57 laps/brakes	1	1m16.533s	16
R	Enrique Bernoldi	Arrows	48 laps/engine	1	1m16.645s	18
R	Olivier Panis	BAR	39 laps/engine	1	1m15.851s	7
R	Jarno Trulli	Renault	36 laps/spun off	2	1m15.885s	8
R	Jacques Villeneuve	BAR	27 laps/gearbox	1	1m16.070s	11
R	Jenson Button	Renault	24 laps/engine	0	1m16.278s	13
R	Allan McNish	Toyota	23 laps/hydraulics	1	1m16.594s	17
R	Mark Webber	Minardi	23 laps/hydraulics	0	1m17.996s	21
R	Heinz-Harald Frentzen	Arrows	18 laps/hydraulics	0	1m16.505s	15
R	Pedro de la Rosa	Jaguar	0 laps/transmission	0	1m17.077s	20
NQ	Alex Yoong	Minardi	-	-	1m19.775s	-

Pole time
M Schumacher, 1m14.389s, 137.550mph/221.355kph

Winner's average speed
130.035mph/209.262kph

Fastest lap
M Schumacher, 1m16.462s, 133.821mph/215.354kph

Lap leaders
M Schumacher, 1–26, 31–47 & 49–67; R Schumacher, 27–29 & 48;
Montoya, 30

Full Gas: Juan Pablo Montoya keeps Michael Schumacher under pressure at the hairpin

HUNGARIAN GP

ANOTHER FERRARI PROCESSION

Ferrari dominated as never before, controlling all before them in Hungary. With the team putting its weight behind helping Rubens Barrichello to finish second in the championship, Michael Schumacher played the supporting role.

New Boy: British driver Anthony Davidson stood in for Alex Yoong at Minardi and made a good impression as he all but matched Mark Webber's pace. However, he spun out of the race

When the red cars lined up first and second on the grid, with Rubens Barrichello on pole for the third time in 2002, and only Ralf Schumacher's Williams vaguely close on time, the race looked a formality for the Brazilian.

The only challenge came from Ralf, but his bid to pass Michael into the first corner was rebuffed. And that was that. Despite driving flat-out throughout, Ralf had a race of his own, as team-mate Juan Pablo Montoya had a problem getting under way and fell back, leaving Giancarlo Fisichella in fourth. Montoya fell to ninth, then later damaged a turning vane on a kerb and struggled even to stay on the track.

On this circuit, where passing is all but impossible, Rubens led all the way save for his pit stops, both times emerging just in front of Michael. Just to show that he could have won the race if he hadn't had to play a supporting role to Rubens, Michael dropped back with five laps to go and slotted in the race's fastest lap, taking almost 4s off Rubens in that one lap alone. Apparently, he was "just having fun"...

The only team to make progress during the race was McLaren, after they'd qualified 10th (David Coulthard) and 11th (Kimi Raikkonen), unable to explain their cars' lack of grip as Bridgestone again lorded it over Michelin. Raikkonen made the better start and demoted not only Coulthard, but also Nick Heidfeld. Latching onto Montoya's tail, the Finn advanced when the Colombian pitted early for repairs. He then moved past Jenson Button when the Renault driver spun off and was sixth behind Jarno Trulli after the first pitstops. Running longer second stints helped Raikkonen to an eventual fourth, with Coulthard fifth ahead of Fisichella.

The Hungarian GP was also notable for three things. Firstly, the announcement by Honda that it would curtail its contract to supply engines to Jordan a year early, with Jordan announcing that it would use Ford power in 2003. Secondly, Arrows failed to show, on the advice of their lawyers as they were in the midst of trying to sort out a takeover bid and sundry financial matters.

Finally, there was the debut of Anthony Davidson who was filling in at Minardi for two races while Alex Yoong stepped back to gather his thoughts after a troubled run. The 23-year-old impressed, even lapping faster than team-mate Mark Webber.

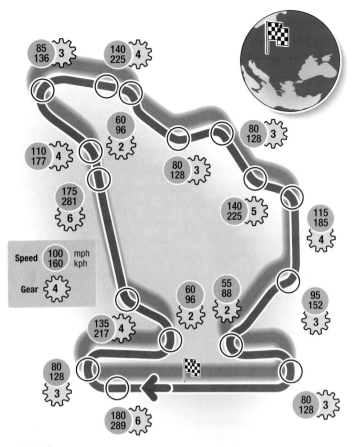

Speed 100 / 160 mph / kph

Gear 4

Pole time
Barrichello, 1m13.333s, 121.258mph/195.136kph

Winner's average speed
112.078mph/180.364kph

Fastest lap
M Schumacher, 1m16.207s, 116.685mph/187.778kph

Lap leaders
Barrichello, 1–31 & 33–77; R Schumacher, 32

HUNGARORING ROUND 13

Date 18 August 2002 **Laps** 77 **Distance** 190.19 miles/306.07km
Weather Hot, dry and bright

RACE RESULTS

Position	Driver	Team	Result	Stops	Qualifying Time	Grid
1	Rubens Barrichello	Ferrari	1h41m49.001s	2	1m13.333s	1
2	Michael Schumacher	Ferrari	1h41m49.435s	2	1m13.392s	2
3	Ralf Schumacher	Williams	1h42m02.357s	2	1m13.746s	3
4	Kimi Raikkonen	McLaren	1h42m18.480s	2	1m15.243s	11
5	David Coulthard	McLaren	1h42m26.801s	2	1m15.223s	10
6	Giancarlo Fisichella	Jordan	1h42m57.805s	2	1m14.880s	5
7	Felipe Massa	Sauber	1h43m02.613s	2	1m15.047s	7
8	Jarno Trulli	Renault	76 laps	2	1m14.980s	6
9	Nick Heidfeld	Sauber	76 laps	2	1m15.129s	8
10	Takuma Sato	Jordan	76 laps	2	1m15.804s	14
11	Juan Pablo Montoya	Williams	76 laps	2	1m14.706s	4
12	Olivier Panis	BAR	76 laps	2	1m15.556s	12
13	Pedro de la Rosa	Jaguar	75 laps	2	1m15.867s	15
14	Allan McNish	Toyota	75 laps	2	1m16.626s	18
15	Mika Salo	Toyota	75 laps*	2	1m16.473s	17
16	Mark Webber	Minardi	75 laps	2	1m17.428s	19
R	Anthony Davidson	Minardi	58 laps/spun off	1	1m17.959s	20
R	Jenson Button	Renault	30 laps/spun off	0	1m15.214s	9
R	Eddie Irvine	Jaguar	23 laps/engine	0	1m16.419s	16
R	Jacques Villeneuve	BAR	20 laps/transmission	0	1m15.583s	13

* Mika Salo had 25s added to his race time for leaving the pitlane when it was not safe to do so

Rubens Rules: Barrichello started on pole and won as he pleased, shadowed by Michael

BELGIAN GP

SCHUMI TAKES A RECORD TENTH

TOUGH OF THE TRACK

Michael Schumacher loves Spa-Francorchamps, and it showed. A superior car and cool weather that suited his Bridgestone tyres let him dominate from start to finish for a record 10th win in a season.

Jim Clark hated Spa-Francorchamps, yet won here four times. **Ayrton Senna** loved it and went one better. His first success high in the Ardennes came with Lotus in 1985, but the other four, coming in consecutive years from 1988 to 1991, were for McLaren. Such was Senna's domination there that his first three McLaren wins came from pole position. In 1991, though, he benefitted from Nigel Mansell (Williams) and Jean Alesi (Ferrari) retirements. Notably, this was also the debut of the driver who would take his mantle: Michael Schumacher.

There was a chink of hope for the opposition – that is to say the teams chasing Ferrari – after qualifying, as the cars in red weren't streets clear around this, the longest circuit on the calendar. Indeed, McLaren's Kimi Raikkonen pushed extremely hard for pole position and split the Ferraris. He might just cause them trouble if he could make a good start.

But he couldn't, and Rubens Barrichello dived past him. The McLaren and Williams drivers had got close in qualifying, but the conditions were cooler on race day and their Michelins, whether soft or hard, never let them match the Bridgestone-shod Ferraris. Indeed, Michael was lapping a good second a lap faster in the first stint.

Except for a late-race warning to back off to ensure engine reliability – after the Ferrari engine in Felipe Massa's Sauber blew – Michael had everything under control, notching up Ferrari's 50th consecutive race to a podium finish, as well as his 10th win of the season, breaking a record that he shared with the watching Nigel Mansell.

Number Ten: Michael's 10th win of the season marked yet another new record, going one better than Nigel Mansell's best, as he excelled on a circuit that he adores

Barrichello doubled Ferrari joy by finishing second, extending his advantage in the race to be overall runner-up behind Michael by two points over Juan Pablo Montoya, who just held off David Coulthard's McLaren. It took some clever use of bi-directional telemetry by Williams in the closing laps to boost his BMW engine's power on the climb from Eau Rouge to Les Combes so that Coulthard couldn't get into his slipstream, before backing the power down for the rest of the lap.

Raikkonen had made McLaren's early running. Yet, having been pushed back to third by Barrichello on the run to the first corner, he then was demoted further when he ran wide at Pouhon on lap 2 and Montoya didn't need to be asked twice.

Ralf Schumacher lost ground in the battle to end the year as runner-up to his brother by finishing a distant fifth. Jarno Trulli had been pushing Ralf hard, but, as in 2001 at Spa, he was deprived of points when his engine blew, handing the place to Eddie Irvine. He and Jaguar team-mate Pedro de la Rosa had both been enjoying improved form due to Jaguar's new front suspension.

For the record, Arrows turned up, didn't practice and left for home on Friday night as the legal procedure of a proposed take-over was sorted out.

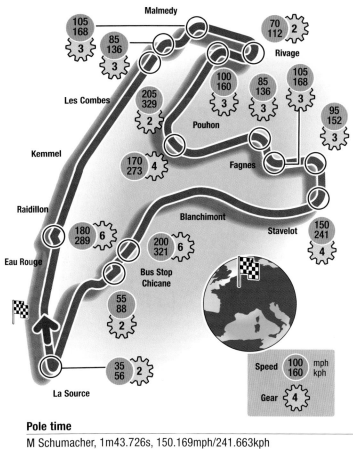

Malmedy
105 168 | 3
85 136 | 3
70 112 | 2 **Rivage**
100 160 | 3
85 136 | 3
105 168 | 3
205 329 | 2 **Les Combes**
95 152 | 3
Pouhon
Kemmel
170 273 | 4
Fagnes
Raidillon
180 289 | 6
Blanchimont
200 321 | 6
Stavelot
150 241 | 4
Eau Rouge
Bus Stop Chicane
55 88 | 2
35 56 | 2
La Source

Speed 100/160 mph/kph
Gear 4

Pole time
M Schumacher, 1m43.726s, 150.169mph/241.663kph

Winner's average speed
140.418mph/225.970kph

Fastest lap
M Schumacher, 1m47.176s, 145.336mph/233.884kph

Lap leaders
M Schumacher, 1–16 & 18–44; Barrichello, 17

SPA-FRANCORCHAMPS ROUND 14

Date 1 September 2002 **Laps** 44 **Distance** 190.37 miles/306.36km
Weather Cool, dry and overcast

RACE RESULTS

Position	Driver	Team	Result	Stops	Qualifying Time	Grid
1	Michael Schumacher	Ferrari	1h21m20.634s	2	1m43.726s	1
2	Rubens Barrichello	Ferrari	1h21m22.611s	2	1m44.335s	3
3	Juan Pablo Montoya	Williams	1h21m39.079s	2	1m44.634s	5
4	David Coulthard	McLaren	1h21m39.992s	2	1m44.759s	6
5	Ralf Schumacher	Williams	1h22m17.074s	2	1m44.348s	4
6	Eddie Irvine	Jaguar	1h22m38.004s	2	1m45.865s	8
7	Mika Salo	Toyota	1h22m38.443s	2	1m45.880s	9
8	Jacques Villeneuve	BAR	1h22m40.489s	2	1m46.403s	12
9	Allan McNish	Toyota	43 laps	2	1m46.485s	13
10	Nick Heidfeld	Sauber	43 laps	2	1m47.272s	18
11	Takuma Sato	Jordan	43 laps	2	1m46.875s	16
12	Olivier Panis	BAR	39 laps/engine	2	1m46.553s	15
R	Giancarlo Fisichella	Jordan	38 laps/engine	1	1m46.508s	14
R	Pedro de la Rosa	Jaguar	37 laps/suspension	2	1m46.056s	11
R	Felipe Massa	Sauber	37 laps/engine	2	1m46.896s	17
R	Kimi Raikkonen	McLaren	35 laps/engine	2	1m44.150s	2
R	Jarno Trulli	Renault	35 laps/engine	2	1m45.386s	7
R	Anthony Davidson	Minardi	17 laps/spun off	1	1m48.170s	20
R	Jenson Button	Renault	10 laps/engine	0	1m45.972s	10
R	Mark Webber	Minardi	4 laps/gearbox	0	1m47.562s	19

Showing Their Colours: Michael's hordes of fans had every reason to wave their flags

>> ITALIAN GP

YET ANOTHER FERRARI STROLL

Williams kidded everyone that they would be able to take the battle to Ferrari at Monza, but the reality was that they couldn't. And so it was left to Rubens Barrichello to take on Michael Schumacher, which he did, and he won.

The Big One: Rubens Barrichello acknowledges that there's absolutely nowhere better for a Ferrari driver to win than on their home turf at Monza. It was the third win of his 2002 campaign

After Ferrari dominated both qualifying and the race at the previous three rounds, Williams struck back on Ferrari's home track, Juan Pablo Montoya claiming pole for Williams by a quarter of a second from Michael Schumacher, with Ralf Schumacher just a fraction behind his brother.

After testing there, it was thought that McLaren would be on the pace, but they weren't, with Kimi Raikkonen 0.4s adrift of Rubens Barrichello and David Coulthard a further 0.6s down. It could have been worse for the Finn after he failed to look into his mirrors at the start of his final out lap and pulled into the path of Takuma Sato's Jordan, leaving it nowhere to go as they approached the second chicane. With two wheels already on the grass, and wheels interlocked, the

Japanese driver made impact and spiralled into the barriers, bringing qualifying to a halt. Fortunately, he was uninjured.

In Raikkonen's defence, it was Sato's third consecutive flying lap – one is the norm, two unusual and three almost unheard of. The result was that the Finn had his fastest lap annulled.

Montoya cut to his right at the start to keep Michael behind him, but Ralf, by running straight, was alongside him as they reached the first chicane. Neither budged and while Montoya slithered through the corner Ralf ran straight on, rejoining in the lead, with the Ferraris third and fourth.

With Michelin's tyres seldom a match for the Bridgestones early in a race, the Williams drivers had to fight hard to keep the red cars behind. They did briefly, but Ralf retired with a blown engine just as he was told to slow to let Montoya through for skipping that first corner, and then Juan Pablo was simply overpowered by the Ferraris.

Barrichello was on a two-stop strategy, Michael on a one-stopper. At one-third distance, the Brazilian pitted and Michael assumed the lead, but Barrichello came out just in front after his second stop and stayed there for his third win of 2002.

With Montoya and Raikkonen failing to finish, Eddie Irvine treated Jaguar to only its second ever podium, this after starting a much-improved fifth. Hard on his heels were the Renaults of Jarno Trulli and Jenson Button, with Olivier Panis claiming sixth by a nose from Coulthard.

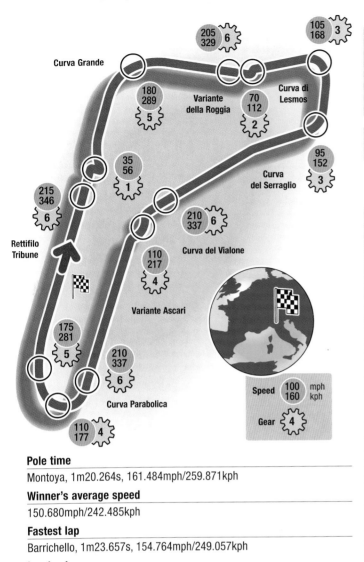

Curva Grande

205 / 329 — 6

105 / 168 — 3

180 / 289 — 5

Variante della Roggia

70 / 112 — 2

Curva di Lesmos

95 / 152 — 3

Curva del Serraglio

35 / 56 — 1

215 / 346 — 6

Rettifilo Tribune

210 / 337 — 6

110 / 217 — 4

Curva del Vialone

Variante Ascari

175 / 281 — 5

210 / 337 — 6

Curva Parabolica

110 / 177 — 4

| Speed | 100 / 160 | mph / kph |
| Gear | 4 | |

Pole time
Montoya, 1m20.264s, 161.484mph/259.871kph

Winner's average speed
150.680mph/242.485kph

Fastest lap
Barrichello, 1m23.657s, 154.764mph/249.057kph

Lap leaders
R Schumacher, 1–3; Montoya, 4; Barrichello, 5–19 & 29–53;
M Schumacher, 20–28

MONZA ROUND 15

Date 15 September 2002 **Laps** 53 **Distance** 190.61 miles/306.74km
Weather Warm, dry and bright

RACE RESULTS

Position	Driver	Team	Result	Stops	Qualifying Time	Grid
1	Rubens Barrichello	Ferrari	1h16m19.982s	2	1m20.706s	4
2	Michael Schumacher	Ferrari	1h16m20.237s	1	1m20.521s	2
3	Eddie Irvine	Jaguar	1h17m12.561s	1	1m21.606s	5
4	Jarno Trulli	Renault	1h17m18.201s	1	1m22.383s	11
5	Jenson Button	Renault	1h17m27.752s	1	1m22.714s	17
6	Olivier Panis	BAR	1h17m28.472s	2	1m22.645s	16
7	David Coulthard	McLaren	1h17m29.029s	2	1m21.803s	7
8	Giancarlo Fisichella	Jordan	1h17m30.874s	1	1m22.515s	12
9	Jacques Villeneuve	BAR	1h17m41.051s	1	1m22.126s	9
10	Nick Heidfeld	Sauber	1h17m42.028s	2	1m22.601s	15
11	Mika Salo	Toyota	52 laps	2	1m22.318s	10
12	Takuma Sato	Jordan	52 laps	1	1m23.166s	18
13	Alex Yoong	Minardi	47 laps	2	1m25.111s	20
R	Juan Pablo Montoya	Williams	30 laps/suspension	1	1m20.264s	1
R	Kimi Raikkonen	McLaren	29 laps/engine	0	1m21.712s*	6
R	Mark Webber	Minardi	20 laps/electrics	1	1m23.794s	19
R	Felipe Massa	Sauber	16 laps/crash damage	0	1m22.565s	14
R	Pedro de la Rosa	Jaguar	15 laps/suspension	0	1m21.960s	8
R	Allan McNish	Toyota	13 laps/suspension	1	1m22.521s	13
R	Ralf Schumacher	Williams	4 laps/engine	0	1m20.542s	3

* Raikkonen's fastest qualifying lap was annulled for reckless driving
that triggered an accident with Takuma Sato that stopped qualifying

Surprise, Surprise: The Jaguar team had clearly made progress, but it still took the retirement of the Williams duo to clear the way for Eddie Irvine to finish third

UNITED STATES GP

MICHAEL UPSETS THE FANS

Michael Schumacher decided, apparently alone, to stage a formation finish with Rubens Barrichello, but he got it wrong and let his team-mate through, hoodwinking the massed American fans.

TOUGH OF THE TRACK

Double world champion **Jim Clark** was the driver who made the greatest impression when a few British-based Formula One teams took on the mighty rear-engined roadsters in the early 1960s in a bid to win the Indianapolis 500. Racing, of course, for Lotus, the flying Scot was kept from winning only by some one-eyed officialdom in 1963. Two years later, Clark and Lotus got it right and lorded it over their American rivals. And to let you know how much this win meant to the British outfit, they even skipped the Monaco GP so that they could race at Indianapolis.

Victor's Spoils: Rubens Barrichello is doused with Champagne after Michael Schumacher surprisingly, but perhaps mistakenly, let him through for an unexpected win on the line.

The gap was just 0.011s, the second closest finish of all time behind the 1971 Italian GP, but the result didn't please the crowds at Indianapolis, who felt that they'd been played with. What Michael had intended to be a dead heat backfired. It would have been vaguely understandable if he'd stuck to this explanation, but he soon changed his story, saying that he'd been trying to give something back to Rubens to make up for what happened at the Austrian GP when Rubens had had to pull over.

With the feeling that Michael and Ferrari were continuing to devalue the sport, leading figures such as Patrick Head of Williams

accused Ferrari of "trivialising" Formula One. Ferrari's Jean Todt denied any team orders, other than that the drivers were asked not to race against each other after their second pit stops. The rest, it seems, was all down to Michael. Indeed, Rubens said after the race that he hadn't wanted to be handed a win like that.

Behind the red cars, David Coulthard ran a one-stop strategy. He closed onto their tails before his stop, but the Ferraris then upped their pace and David had to back off in his second stint as McLaren feared his engine might blow like Kimi Raikkonen's. With Rubens seemingly making no impression on

Michael, although running close behind, the fans' eyes turned to the progress of Juan Pablo Montoya as he closed in on Coulthard.

The Colombian was in a hurry, as his race was affected adversely at the start of the second lap when he made a move past Williams team-mate Ralf Schumacher, only for Ralf to clip a kerb, spin and collide with him. Ralf dropped to a distant last as he pitted for a new rear wing; Juan Pablo fell to seventh. He could possibly have made it by into third – especially with Coulthard backing off – but he misread his pit board and pitted early, still with fuel aboard.

Fifth place went to Jarno Trulli, who started his Renault from eighth place on the grid. A race with Jacques Villeneuve shook out in his favour as the Canadian pitted twice to Jarno's once. Jacques brought his BAR home behind him in sixth for the final point.

Most upset of all, though, were Jaguar, who were disappointingly uncompetitive, especially after Eddie Irvine's third-place finish at Monza. He finished tenth, but it was worse for Pedro de la Rosa. After his transmission failed over-zealous marshals advised him to vault over the trackside barriers, which he did, straight into a water-filled culvert...

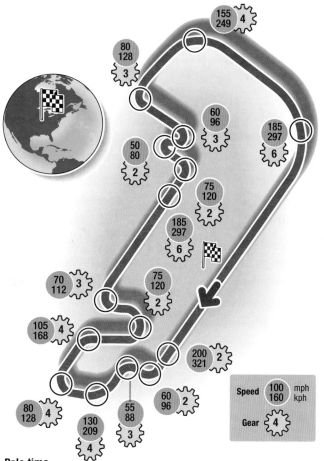

Speed 100 / 160 mph / kph

Gear 4

Pole time

M Schumacher, 1m10.790s, 132.471mph/213.182kph

Winner's average speed

125.197mph/201.475kph

Fastest lap

Barrichello, 1m12.738s, 128.923mph/207.473kph

Lap leaders

M Schumacher, 1–26, 29–48, 51–72; Barrichello, 27–28, 49–50, 73

INDIANAPOLIS ROUND 16

Date: 29 September 2002 **Laps:** 73 **Distance** 190.16 miles/306.02km
Weather: Warm, dry and bright

RACE RESULTS

Position	Driver	Team	Result	Stops	Qualify Time	Grid
1	Rubens Barrichello	Ferrari	1h31m07.934s	2	1m11.058s	2
2	Michael Schumacher	Ferrari	1h31m07.945s	2	1m10.790s	1
3	David Coulthard	McLaren	1h31m15.733s	1	1m11.413s	3
4	Juan Pablo Montoya	Williams	1h31m17.845s	1	1m11.414s	4
5	Jarno Trulli	Renault	1h32m04.781s	1	1m11.888s	8
6	Jacques Villeneuve	BAR	1h32m06.146s	2	1m11.738s	7
7	Giancarlo Fisichella	Jordan	72 laps	1	1m11.902s	9
8	Jenson Button	Renault	72 laps	1	1m12.401s	14
9	Nick Heidfeld	Sauber	72 laps	2	1m11.953s	10
10	Eddie Irvine	Jaguar	72 laps	1	1m12.282s	13
11	Takuma Sato	Jordan	72 laps	2	1m12.647s	15
12	Olivier Panis	BAR	72 laps	2	1m12.161s	12
13	Heinz-Harald Frentzen	Sauber	71 laps	2	1m12.083s	11
14	Mika Salo	Toyota	71 laps	2	1m13.213s	19
15	Allan McNish	Toyota	71 laps	1	1m12.723s	16
16	Ralf Schumacher	Williams	71 laps	1	1m11.587s	5
R	Kimi Raikkonen	McLaren	50 laps/engine	1	1m11.633s	6
R	Alex Yoong	Minardi	46 laps/engine	1	1m13.809s	20
R	Mark Webber	Minardi	38 laps/power steering	-	1m13.128s	18
R	Pedro de la Rosa	Jaguar	27 laps/transmission	-	1m12.739s	17

Room For More: The raceday crowd was good, but there were seats aplenty to spare in the gigantic grandstands when the cars went out to practice on the Friday.

>> JAPANESE GP

YELLOW FEVER

Michael Schumacher extended the record for Grand Prix wins in one season to 11, but the race will be remembered, by Japanese fans at least, for Takuma Sato's drive that culminated in fifth place.

First, the figures: Ferrari claimed its fifth consecutive 1–2 finish; Michael Schumacher completed the season with 11 wins, five seconds and one third – an astonishing and unbeatable feat of a podium finish in every race – and a record 144 points; Ferrari's total of 221 Constructors' Cup points was precisely equal to that scored by all the other teams put together. This result also made Schumacher and Rubens Barrichello the most successful partnership in Formula One history, surpassing – in four seasons – the points tally collected by David Coulthard and Mika Hakkinen in seven years together at McLaren.

Now the human story. Although the red cars started from the front row and finished nose-to-tail in another formation finish, it was what happened behind that had the crowd waving their flags throughout the race before standing up and cheering to the echo at the race's end. Takuma Sato's future at Jordan was in the balance – contract for 2003 or not – given his often spectacular, but pointless maiden Formula One season. Yet his fans turned up in droves, delighted to have one of their own in the reckoning.

Honda brought along an upgraded qualifying engine, but it blew, so Takuma had to make do with the previous specification. This left Takuma to tussle race-long with the Renault pair, Jarno Trulli and Jenson Button. A crafty alteration at the first of his two pitstops helped with handling and Takuma led them when he emerged from his second stop. He was heading for sixth place and his first ever point, thanks in part to Coulthard's early retirement. However, with fewer than five laps to go, Ralf Schumacher parked his smoking Williams. So Takuma was fifth. The crowd went wild, as did Eddie Jordan because his team ended the year sixth overall, having overhauled non-scorers Jaguar.

Kimi Raikkonen followed home the Ferraris, McLaren's second driver overcoming a late-race scare when his engine stuttered briefly. Juan Pablo Montoya was a lacklustre fourth for Williams. The final point went to Jenson Button, in sixth place, on his final outing for Renault.

The luckiest driver at Suzuka was not Sato, but Allan McNish, who failed a medical inspection and could not race, following a massive accident that ended up with his Toyota at rest on the banking, having speared through the barriers at 150mph on the exit of the fearsome 130R. The plucky Scot would not have wished to bring his season with the Japanese team to a close this way. Team-mate Mika Salo ran the race, though, finishing eighth behind Nick Heidfeld's Sauber.

Thus, Ferrari's record-breaking 2002 campaign finally come to an end, leaving the other teams fighting either to develop superior cars for 2003 or simply for survival.

TOUGH OF THE TRACK

Until last October, no Japanese driver since Aguri Suzuki in 1990 had shown well enough to be considered a hero at Suzuka. However, the locals must have known something, as fully two grandstands were filled by **Takuma Sato** fans. After the Jordan driver qualified a season-best seventh, the stalls sold out of his caps. When he out-raced the Renaults to finish fifth, Takuma's reception was far greater than winner Michael Schumacher's. Indeed, the result was rather less expected…

The Fans' Favourite: The packed grandstands at Suzuka went wild every time their new local hero, Takuma Sato, drove past. They then went absolutely and deleriously berserk when he drove his Jordan to a fighting fifth-place finish for his only championship points of the season.

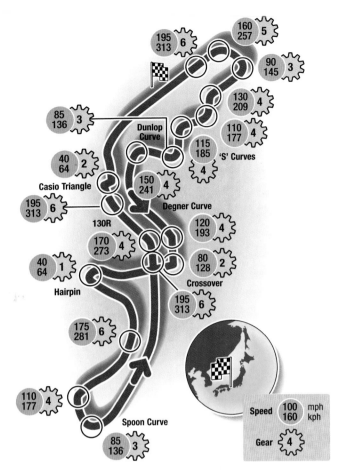

Track map labels

- 195 / 313 — 6
- 160 / 257 — 5
- 90 / 145 — 3
- 130 / 209 — 4
- 85 / 136 — 3
- **Dunlop Curve**
- 110 / 177 — 4
- 115 / 185 — 4
- **'S' Curves**
- 40 / 64 — 2
- 150 / 241 — 4
- **Casio Triangle**
- **Degner Curve**
- 195 / 313 — 6
- 120 / 193 — 4
- **130R**
- 170 / 273 — 4
- 80 / 128 — 2
- 40 / 64 — 1
- **Crossover**
- **Hairpin**
- 195 / 313 — 6
- 175 / 281 — 6
- 110 / 177 — 4
- **Spoon Curve**
- 85 / 136 — 3

Speed 100 / 160 mph / kph
Gear 4

Pole times
M Schumacher, 1m31.317s, 142.599mph/229.481kph

Winner's average speed
132.137mph/212.644kph

Fastest lap
M Schumacher, 1m36.125s, 135.467mph/218.003kph

Lap leaders
M Schumacher, 1–20, 22–53; Barrichello, 21

 SUZUKA ROUND 17

Date 13 October 2002 **Laps** 53 **Distance** 191.59 miles/308.32km
Weather Warm, dry and bright

RACE RESULTS

Position	Driver	Team	Result	Stops	Qualify Time	Grid
1	Michael Schumacher	Ferrari	1h26m59.698s	2	1m31.317s	1
2	Rubens Barrichello	Ferrari	1h27m00.205s	2	1m31.749s	2
3	Kimi Raikkonen	McLaren	1h27m22.990s	2	1m32.197s	4
4	Juan Pablo Montoya	Williams	1h27m35.973s	2	1m32.507s	6
5	Takuma Sato	Jordan	1h28m22.392s	2	1m33.090s	7
6	Jenson Button	Renault	52 laps	2	1m33.429s	10
7	Nick Heidfeld	Sauber	52 laps	2	1m33.553s	12
8	Mika Salo	Toyota	52 laps	2	1m33.742s	13
9	Eddie Irvine	Jaguar	52 laps	2	1m33.915s	14
10	Mark Webber	Minardi	51 laps	2	1m35.958s	19
11	Ralf Schumacher	Williams	48 laps/engine	2	1m32.444s	5
R	Pedro de la Rosa	Jaguar	39 laps/transmission	2	1m34.227s	17
R	Giancarlo Fisichella	Jordan	37 laps/engine	2	1m33.276s	8
R	Jarno Trulli	Renault	32 laps/engine	1	1m33.547s	11
R	Jacques Villeneuve	BAR	27 laps/engine	1	1m33.349s	9
R	Alex Yoong	Minardi	14 laps/spun off	-	1m36.267s	20
R	Olivier Panis	BAR	8 laps/electronics	2	1m34.192s	16
R	David Coulthard	McLaren	7 laps/electronics	-	1m32.088s	3
R	Felipe Massa	Sauber	3 laps/spun off	-	1m33.979s	15
NS	Allan McNish	Toyota	-/leg injury	-	1m35.191s	18

The Final Podium Of The Year: Ferrari's Rubens Barrichello and McLaren's Kimi Raikkonen flank the record-extending race winner, Michael Schumacher.

Driver	Nationality	Car-Engine	1 March 4, Australian GP	2 March 18, Malaysian GP	3 April 1, Brazilian GP	4 April 15, San Marino GP	5 April 29, Spanish GP
Michael Schumacher	GER	Ferrari F2001	1	3P	-	-	-
		Ferrari F2002	-	-	1	1P	1PF
Rubens Barrichello	BRA	Ferrari F2001	RP	R	R	-	
		Ferrari F2002	-	-	-	2F	R
Juan Pablo Montoya	COL	Williams-BMW FW24	2	2F	5PF	4	2
Ralf Schumacher	GER	Williams-BMW FW24	R	1	2	3	11
David Coulthard	GBR	McLaren-Mercedes MP4-17	R	R	3	6	3
Kimi Raikkonen	FIN	McLaren-Mercedes MP4-17	3F	R	12	R	R
Jenson Button	GBR	Renault R202	R	4	4	5	12
Jarno Trulli	ITA	Renault R202	R	R	R	9	10
Eddie Irvine	GBR	Jaguar R3	4	R	7	R	R
Nick Heidfeld	GER	Sauber-Petronas C21	R	5	R	10	4
Giancarlo Fisichella	ITA	Jordan-Honda EJ12	R	13	R	R	R
Felipe Massa	BRA	Sauber-Petronas C21	R	6	R	8	5
Jacques Villeneuve	CDN	BAR-Honda 004	R	8	10	7	7
Olivier Panis	FRA	BAR-Honda 004	R	R	R	R	R
Mark Webber	AUS	Minardi-Asiatech PS02	5	R	11	11	W
Mika Salo	FIN	Toyota TF102	6	12	6	R	9
Heinz-Harald Frentzen	GER	Arrows-Cosworth A23	D	11	R	R	6
		Sauber-Petronas C21	-	-	-	-	-
Takuma Sato	JAP	Jordan-Honda EJ12	R	9	9	R	R
Allan McNish	GBR	Toyota TF102	R	7	R	R	8
Alex Yoong	MAL	Minardi-Asiatech PS02	7	R	13	NQ	W
Pedro de la Rosa	ESP	Jaguar R3	8	10	8	R	R
Enrique Bernoldi	BRA	Arrows-Cosworth A23	D	R	R	R	R
Anthony Davidson	GBR	Minardi-Asiatech PS02	-	-	-	-	-

Scoring System

First	**10 points**
Second	**6 points**
Third	**4 points**
Fourth	**3 points**
Fifth	**2 points**
Sixth	**1 point**

Symbols

D	disqualified
F	fastest lap
NQ	non-qualifier
NS	non-starter
P	pole position
R	retired
W	withdrawn

Constuctor

	Constructor	1	2	3	4	5
1	Ferrari	10	4	10	16	10
2	Williams-BMW	6	16	8	7	6
3	McLaren-Mercedes	4	-	4	1	4
4	Renault	-	3	3	2	-
5	Sauber-Petronas	-	3	-	-	5
6	Jordan-Honda	-	-	-	-	-
7	Jaguar-Cosworth	3	-	-	-	-
8	BAR-Honda	-	-	-	-	-
9	Minardi-Asiatech	2	-	-	-	-
10	Toyota	1	-	1	-	-
11	Arrows-Cosworth	-	-	-	-	1

6 May 13, Austrian GP	7 May 27, Monaco GP	8 June 10, Canadian GP	9 June 24, European GP	10 July 1, French GP	11 July 15, British GP	12 July 29, German GP	13 August 19, Hungarian GP	14 September 2, Belgian GP	15 September 16, Italian GP	16 September 30, United States GP	17 October 14, Japanese GP	Points Total
-	-	-	-	-	-	-	-	-	-	-	-	-
1F	2	1	2F	1	1	1PF	2F	1PF	2	2P	1PF	144
-	-	-	-	-	-	-	-	-	-	-	-	-
2P	7F	3	1	2F	R	4	1P	2	1F	1F	2	77
3	RP	RPF	RP	3P	4P	2	11	3	RP	4	4	50
4	3	7	4	8	5	3	3	5	R	16	11	42
6	1	2	R	10	3F	5	5	4	7	3	R	41
R	R	4	3	R	2	R	4	R	R	R	3	24
7	R	15	6	12	6	R	R	5	5	8	6	14
R	4	6	8	R	R	R	8	R	4	5	R	9
R	9	R	R	R	R	R	R	6	3	10	9	8
R	8	12	7	6	7	6	9	10	10	9	7	7
5	5	5	R	7	W	R	6	R	8	7	R	7
8	R	9	6	9	R	7	7	R	R	9	R	4
10	R	R	12	4	R	R	R	R	9	6	R	4
R	R	8	9	5	R	R	12	R	6	12	R	3
12	11	11	15	R	8	R	16	R	R	R	10	2
8	R	R	R	R	R	9	15	7	11	14	8	2
11	6	13	13	R	NQ	R	-	-	-	-	-	2
-	-	-	-	-	-	-	-	-	-	13	-	
R	R	10	16	R	R	8	10	11	12	11	5	2
9	R	R	14	R	11	R	14	9	R	15	NS	0
R	R	14	R	NQ	10	NQ	-	-	13	R	R	0
R	10	R	11	11	9	R	13	R	R	R	R	0
R	12	R	10	R	NQ	R	R	-	-	-	-	0
-	-	-	-	-	-	-	R	R	-	-	-	0

Note: **Drivers are listed according to their total points at the end of the season.**

6 May 13, Austrian GP	7 May 27, Monaco GP	8 June 10, Canadian GP	9 June 24, European GP	10 July 1, French GP	11 July 15, British GP	12 July 29, German GP	13 August 19, Hungarian GP	14 September 2, Belgian GP	15 September 16, Italian GP	16 September 30, United States GP	17 October 14, Japanese GP	Points Total
16	6	14	16	16	10	13	16	16	16	16	16	221
7	4	-	3	4	5	10	4	6	-	3	3	92
1	10	9	4	-	10	2	5	3	-	4	4	65
-	3	1	2	-	1	-	-	-	5	2	1	23
-	-	-	1	1	-	1	-	-	-	-	-	11
2	2	2	-	-	-	-	1	-	-	-	2	9
-	-	-	-	-	-	-	-	1	4	-	-	8
-	-	-	-	5	-	-	-	-	1	1	-	7
-	-	-	-	-	-	-	-	-	-	-	-	2
-	-	-	-	-	-	-	-	-	-	-	2	2
-	1	-	-	-	-	-	-	-	-	-	-	2

>> F1 RECORDS

GRAND PRIX CHRONOLOGY

1950 First FIA World Championship for cars with 1.5-litre supercharged or 4.5-litre normally-aspirated engines. Indy 500 is included as a round, but no F1 teams attend.

1951 BRM and Girling introduce disc brakes.

1952 Championship is run for cars with 2-litre normally-aspirated engines, that's to say F2 cars.

1954 Maximum engine capacity increased to 2.5-litres. Supercharged engines are re-admitted if less than 750cc. Minimum race duration of 500km or three hours.

1958 Minimum race duration of 300km or two hours imposed. Stirling Moss scores first rear-engined win.

Advantage BRM: Graham Hill's victory in the Italian GP helped towards winning the drivers' title in 1962, starting a British winning streak.

1960 Final win for a rear-engined car. Last year for Indy 500 in championship.

1961 Maximum engine capacity is 1.5-litre normally-aspirated, with a weight limit of 450kg. Commercial fuel becomes mandatory in place of Avgas. Supercharged engines are banned.

1962 Monocoque Lotus revolutionizes F1.

1966 Debut season for 3-litre formula with a 500kg weight limit.

1967 Ford Cosworth DFV, the most successful F1 engine ever, wins on debut. Aerodynamic wings seen for first time above engine.

1968 Wings put on supports to become spoilers, both above front and rear axles. Gold Leaf Lotus heralds age of sponsorship.

1969 Onboard extinguishers and roll-hoops made mandatory. Four-wheel drive is toyed with. Moveable aerodynamic devices are banned mid-year.

1970 Bag fuel tanks made mandatory. Minimum weight is 530kg.

1971 Slick tyres are introduced. Lotus tries a gas turbine engine.

1972 Engines with more than 12 cylinders are banned.

1973 Maximum fuel tank size is 250 litres, minimum weight is 575kg. Breathable air driver safety system introduced.

1974 Rear wing overhang limited to 1m behind rear axle.

1975 Hesketh and Hill try carbonfibre aerodynamic parts.

1976 Rear wing overhang cut back to 80cm. Tall air boxes banned from Spanish GP. McLaren introduces Kevlar and Nomex in its structure.

1977 Renault's RS01 brings 1.5-litre turbo engines to F1. Lotus introduces ground effect.

1978 Brabham's "fan car" wins Swedish GP and is banned. Tyrrell tests active suspension.

1979 Renault's Jean-Pierre Jabouille scores first turbo win.

1980 Brabham introduces carbon brake discs.

1981 McLaren's carbonfibre monocoque revolutionizes F1 car construction. Sliding skirts are banned and 6cm ground clearance enforced. Minimum weight now 585kg.

1982 Survival cells made mandatory. Brabham introduces refuelling pit stops.

1983 Brabham's Nelson Piquet and BMW become first turbo world champions. Ground effect is banned and flat bottoms introduced. Michele Alboreto scores last DFV win. Minimum weight cut to 540kg.

1984 Fuel tank cut to 220 litres. Mid-race refuelling banned.

1985 Crash-tested nose box becomes mandatory.

1986 Normally-aspirated engines are banned as F1 goes all-turbo, with maximum fuel capacity of 195 litres.

1987 3.5-litre normally-aspirated engines introduced alongside turbos, with 500kg minimum weight limit against turbos' 540kg. Turbos limited to 4 bar boost.

1988 Pop-off boost limited to 2.5 bar and fuel allowance for turbo cars cut to 150 litres. Drivers' feet must be behind front axle.

1989 Turbo engines banned and fuel tank capacity cut to 150 litres for normally-aspirated engines. Ferrari introduces semi-automatic gearboxes.

1992 Top teams use driver aids such as active suspension, traction control and anti-lock brakes.

1994 Driver aids outlawed. Refuelling pit stops permitted again. Ayrton Senna and Roland Ratzenberger die at Imola, triggering rule changes and introducing more chicanes to slow cars at fast circuits.

1995 Engine capacity cut to 3.0 litres. Wing size reduced to cut downforce.

1996 Higher cockpit-side protection made mandatory. Aerodynamic suspension parts banned.

1998 Chassis made narrower. Grooved tyres introduced and slicks banned in order to slow the cars.

1999 Extra groove is added to front and rear tyres.

2001 Traction control is permitted from Spanish GP onwards.

2002 Ferrari dominance spurs FIA to seek solution to make racing more entertaining for 2003, but the bulk of the suggestions are rejected "to keep Formula One pure".

WORLD CHAMPIONS

DRIVERS

Year	Driver	Constructor
1950	Giuseppe Farina	Alfa Romeo
1951	Juan Manuel Fangio	Alfa Romeo
1952	Alberto Ascari	Ferrari
1953	Alberto Ascari	Ferrari
1954	Juan Manuel Fangio	Maserati/Merc
1955	Juan Manuel Fangio	Mercedes
1956	Juan Manuel Fangio	Ferrari
1957	Juan Manuel Fangio	Maserati
1958	Mike Hawthorn	Ferrari
1959	Jack Brabham	Cooper
1960	Jack Brabham	Cooper
1961	Phil Hill	Ferrari
1962	Graham Hill	BRM
1963	Jim Clark	Lotus
1964	John Surtees	Ferrari
1965	Jim Clark	Lotus
1966	Jack Brabham	Brabham
1967	Denny Hulme	Brabham
1968	Graham Hill	Lotus
1969	Jackie Stewart	Matra
1970	Jochen Rindt	Lotus
1971	Jackie Stewart	Tyrrell
1972	Emerson Fittipaldi	Lotus
1973	Jackie Stewart	Tyrrell
1974	Emerson Fittipaldi	McLaren
1975	Niki Lauda	Ferrari
1976	James Hunt	McLaren
1977	Niki Lauda	Ferrari
1978	Mario Andretti	Lotus
1979	Jody Scheckter	Ferrari
1980	Alan Jones	Williams
1981	Nelson Piquet	Brabham
1982	Keke Rosberg	Williams
1983	Nelson Piquet	Brabham
1984	Niki Lauda	McLaren
1985	Alain Prost	McLaren
1986	Alain Prost	McLaren
1987	Nelson Piquet	Williams
1988	Ayrton Senna	McLaren
1989	Alain Prost	McLaren
1990	Ayrton Senna	McLaren
1991	Ayrton Senna	McLaren
1992	Nigel Mansell	Williams
1993	Alain Prost	Williams
1994	Michael Schumacher	Benetton
1995	Michael Schumacher	Benetton
1996	Damon Hill	Williams
1997	Jacques Villeneuve	Williams
1998	Mika Hakkinen	McLaren
1999	Mika Hakkinen	McLaren
2000	Michael Schumacher	Ferrari
2001	Michael Schumacher	Ferrari
2002	Michael Schumacher	Ferrari

CONSTRUCTORS

Year	Constructor
1958	Vanwall
1959	Cooper-Climax
1960	Cooper-Climax
1961	Ferrari
1962	BRM
1963	Lotus-Climax
1964	Ferrari
1965	Lotus-Climax
1966	Brabham-Repco
1967	Brabham-Repco
1968	Lotus-Ford DFV
1969	Matra-Ford DFV
1970	Lotus-Ford DFV
1971	Tyrrell-Ford DFV
1972	Lotus-Ford DFV
1973	Lotus-Ford DFV
1974	McLaren-Ford DFV
1975	Ferrari
1976	Ferrari
1977	Ferrari
1978	Lotus-Ford DFV
1979	Ferrari
1980	Williams-Ford DFV
1981	Williams-Ford DFV
1982	Ferrari
1983	Ferrari
1984	McLaren-TAG
1985	McLaren-TAG
1986	Williams-Honda
1987	Williams-Honda
1988	McLaren-Honda
1989	McLaren-Honda
1990	McLaren-Honda
1991	McLaren-Honda
1992	Williams-Renault
1993	Williams-Renault
1994	Williams-Renault
1995	Benetton-Renault
1996	Williams-Renault
1997	Williams-Renault
1998	McLaren-Mercedes
1999	Ferrari
2000	Ferrari
2001	Ferrari
2002	Ferrari

National Pride: Nigel Mansell was truly delighted to win on home ground at Silverstone in 1992 as the result set him up for his long-awaited World Drivers' Championship title.

Ferrari Rules: The massed ranks of the *tifosi* are passionate about supporting the team that tops almost every record in Formula One history.

MOST GRANDS PRIX STARTS

DRIVERS

256	Riccardo Patrese	(ITA)		Derek Warwick	(GBR)
210	Gerhard Berger	(AUT)	146	Carlos Reutemann	(ARG)
208	Andrea de Cesaris	(ITA)	144	Emerson Fittipaldi	(BRA)
204	Nelson Piquet	(BRA)	143	Heinz-Harald Frentzen	(GER)
201	Jean Alesi	(FRA)	141	David Coulthard	(GBR)
199	Alain Prost	(FRA)	135	Jean-Pierre Jarier	(FRA)
194	Michele Alboreto	(ITA)	132	Clay Regazzoni	(SUI)
187	Nigel Mansell	(GBR)	128	Mario Andretti	(USA)
179	Michael Schumacher	(GER)	126	Jack Brabham	(AUS)
176	Graham Hill	(GBR)	125	Olivier Panis	(FRA)
175	Jacques Laffite	(FRA)	123	Ronnie Peterson	(SWE)
171	Niki Lauda	(AUT)	119	Pierluigi Martini	(ITA)
164	Rubens Barrichello	(BRA)	116	Jacky Ickx	(BEL)
163	Thierry Boutsen	(BEL)		Damon Hill	(GBR)
162	Mika Hakkinen	(FIN)		Alan Jones	(AUS)
	Johnny Herbert	(GBR)		Jacques Villeneuve	(CDN)
161	Ayrton Senna	(BRA)	114	Keke Rosberg	(FIN)
158	Martin Brundle	(GBR)		Patrick Tambay	(FRA)
152	John Watson	(GBR)	112	Denny Hulme	(NZL)
149	Rene Arnoux	(FRA)		Jody Scheckter	(RSA)
147	Eddie Irvine	(GBR)			

CONSTRUCTORS

670	Ferrari	394	Brabham		Jordan
543	McLaren	383	Arrows	163	Sauber
490	Lotus	317	Benetton	140	Renault
462	Williams	288	Minardi	132	Osella
418	Tyrrell	230	March	129	Cooper
409	Prost	197	BRM		

MOST WINS

DRIVERS

64	Michael Schumacher	(GER)		David Coulthard	(GBR)
51	Alain Prost	(FRA)		Alan Jones	(AUS)
41	Ayrton Senna	(BRA)		Carlos Reutemann	(ARG)
31	Nigel Mansell	(GBR)	11	Jacques Villeneuve	(CDN)
27	Jackie Stewart	(GBR)	10	Gerhard Berger	(AUT)
25	Jim Clark	(GBR)		James Hunt	(GBR)
	Niki Lauda	(AUT)		Ronnie Peterson	(SWE)
24	Juan Manuel Fangio	(ARG)		Jody Scheckter	(RSA)
23	Nelson Piquet	(BRA)	8	Denny Hulme	(NZL)
22	Damon Hill	(GBR)		Jacky Ickx	(BEL)
20	Mika Hakkinen	(FIN)	7	Rene Arnoux	(FRA)
16	Stirling Moss	(GBR)	6	Tony Brooks	(GBR)
14	Jack Brabham	(AUS)		Jacques Laffite	(FRA)
	Emerson Fittipaldi	(BRA)		Riccardo Patrese	(FRA)
	Graham Hill	(GBR)		Jochen Rindt	(AUT)
13	Alberto Ascari	(ITA)		John Surtees	(GBR)
12	Mario Andretti	(USA)		Gilles Villeneuve	(CDN)

CONSTRUCTORS

159	Ferrari	15	Renault		March
135	McLaren	10	Alfa Romeo		Wolf
107	Williams	9	Ligier	2	Honda
79	Lotus		Maserati	1	Eagle
35	Brabham		Matra		Hesketh
27	Benetton		Mercedes		Penske
23	Tyrrell		Vanwall		Porsche
17	BRM	3	Jordan		Shadow
16	Cooper				Stewart

MOST WINS IN ONE SEASON

DRIVERS

11	M Schumacher (GER)	2002		Ayrton Senna	(BRA)	1991
9	Nigel Mansell (GBR)	1992		J Villeneuve	(CDN)	1997
	M Schumacher (GER)	1995	6	Mario Andretti	(USA)	1978
	M Schumacher (GER)	2000		Alberto Ascari	(ITA)	1952
	M Schumacher (GER)	2001		Jim Clark	(GBR)	1965
8	Mika Hakkinen (FIN)	1998		Juan M Fangio	(ARG)	1954
	Damon Hill (GBR)	1996		Damon Hill	(GBR)	1994
	M Schumacher (GER)	1994		James Hunt	(GBR)	1976
	Ayrton Senna (BRA)	1988		Nigel Mansell	(GBR)	1987
7	Jim Clark (GBR)	1963		M Schumacher	(GER)	1998
	Alain Prost (FRA)	1984		Ayrton Senna	(BRA)	1989
	Alain Prost (FRA)	1988		Ayrton Senna	(BRA)	1990
	Alain Prost (FRA)	1993				

CONSTRUCTORS

15	Ferrari	2002		McLaren	1991	Ferrari	1976
	McLaren	1988		Williams	1997	Ferrari	1979
12	McLaren	1984	7	Ferrari	1952	Ferrari	1990
	Williams	1996		Ferrari	1953	Ferrari	1996
11	Benetton	1995		Lotus	1963	Ferrari	1998
10	Ferrari	2000		Lotus	1973	Ferrari	1999
	McLaren	1989		McLaren	1999	Lotus	1965
	Williams	1992		McLaren	2000	Lotus	1970
	Williams	1993		Tyrrell	1971	McLaren	1976
9	Ferrari	2001		Williams	1991	McLaren	1985
	McLaren	1998		Williams	1994	McLaren	1990
	Williams	1986	6	Alfa Romeo	1950	Vanwall	1958
	Williams	1987		Alfa Romeo	1951	Williams	1980
8	Benetton	1994		Cooper	1960		
	Lotus	1978		Ferrari	1975		

MOST CONSECUTIVE WINS

9	Alberto Ascari (ITA)	1952/53		Damon Hill (GBR)	1995/96
6	M Schumacher (GER)	2000/01		Alain Prost (FRA)	1993
5	Jack Brabham (AUS)	1960		Jochen Rindt (AUT)	1970
	Jim Clark (GBR)	1965		M Schumacher (GER)	1994
	Nigel Mansell (GBR)	1992		M Schumacher (GER)	2002
4	Jack Brabham (AUS)	1966		Ayrton Senna (BRA)	1988
	Jim Clark (GBR)	1963		Ayrton Senna (BRA)	1991
	Juan M Fangio (ARG)	1953/54			

Ferrari's Hero: Michael Schumacher extended his record for wins in a season last year, to 11, from 17 races. It was outright domination, because he finished on the podium in all of the other races.

STARTS WITHOUT A WIN

208	Andrea de Cesaris (ITA)	109	Philippe Alliot (FRA)
158	Martin Brundle (GBR)	108	Giancarlo Fisichella (ITA)
147	Derek Warwick (GBR)	99	Pedro Diniz (BRA)
135	Jean-Pierre Jarier (FRA)	97	Chris Amon (NZL)
132	Eddie Cheever (USA)		Jarno Trulli (ITA)
119	Pierluigi Martini (ITA)	95	Ukyo Katayama (JAP)
111	Mika Salo (FIN)	93	Ivan Capelli (ITA)

MOST FASTEST LAPS

DRIVERS

50	Michael Schumacher (GER)			Ayrton Senna	(BRA)
41	Alain Prost	(FRA)	18	David Coulthard	(GBR)
30	Nigel Mansell	(GBR)	15	Clay Regazzoni	(SUI)
28	Jim Clark	(GBR)		Jackie Stewart	(GBR)
25	Mika Hakkinen	(FIN)	14	Jacky Ickx	(BEL)
	Niki Lauda	(AUT)	13	Alberto Ascari	(ITA)
23	Juan Manuel Fangio (ARG)			Alan Jones	(AUS)
	Nelson Piquet	(BRA)		Riccardo Patrese	(ITA)
21	Gerhard Berger	(AUT)	12	Rene Arnoux	(FRA)
20	Stirling Moss	(GBR)		Jack Brabham	(AUS)
19	Damon Hill	(GBR)	11	John Surtees	(GBR)

CONSTRUCTORS

158	Ferrari	20	Tyrrell	12	Matra
122	Williams	18	Renault	11	Prost
109	McLaren	15	BRM	9	Mercedes
71	Lotus		Maserati	7	March
40	Brabham	14	Alfa Romeo	6	Vanwall
35	Benetton	13	Cooper		

MOST POLE POSITIONS

DRIVERS

65	Ayrton Senna	(BRA)	14	Alberto Ascari	(ITA)
50	Michael Schumacher	(GER)		James Hunt	(GBR)
33	Jim Clark	(GBR)		Ronnie Peterson	(SWE)
	Alain Prost	(FRA)	13	Jack Brabham	(AUS)
32	Nigel Mansell	(GBR)		Graham Hill	(GBR)
29	Juan Manuel Fangio	(ARG)		Jacky Ickx	(BEL)
26	Mika Hakkinen	(FIN)		Jacques Villeneuve	(CDN)
24	Niki Lauda	(AUT)	12	Gerhard Berger	(AUT)
	Nelson Piquet	(BRA)		David Coulthard	(GBR)
20	Damon Hill	(GBR)	10	Juan Pablo Montoya	(COL)
18	Mario Andretti	(USA)		Jochen Rindt	(AUT)
	Rene Arnoux	(FRA)	8	Riccardo Patrese	(ITA)
17	Jackie Stewart	(GBR)		John Surtees	(GBR)
16	Stirling Moss	(GBR)			

CONSTRUCTORS

158	Ferrari	14	Tyrrell	7	Vanwall
119	Williams	12	Alfa Romeo	5	March
112	McLaren	11	BRM	4	Matra
107	Lotus		Cooper	3	Shadow
39	Brabham	10	Maserati	2	Jordan
31	Renault	9	Prost		Lancia
16	Benetton	8	Mercedes	1	Jaguar

IN ONE SEASON, DRIVERS

14	Nigel Mansell	(GBR)	1992		Nelson Piquet	(BRA)	1984
13	Alain Prost	(FRA)	1993		M Schumacher	(GER)	2000
	Ayrton Senna	(BRA)	1988	8	Mario Andretti	(USA)	1978
	Ayrton Senna	(BRA)	1989		James Hunt	(GBR)	1976
11	Mika Hakkinen	(FIN)	1999		Nigel Mansell	(GBR)	1987
	M Schumacher	(GER)	2001		Ayrton Senna	(BRA)	1986
10	Ayrton Senna	(BRA)	1990		Ayrton Senna	(BRA)	1991
	J Villeneuve	(CDN)	1997	7	Mario Andretti	(USA)	1977
9	Mika Hakkinen	(FIN)	1998		Jim Clark	(GBR)	1963
	Damon Hill	(GBR)	1996		Damon Hill	(GBR)	1995
	Niki Lauda	(AUT)	1974		Juan P Montoya	(COL)	2002
	Niki Lauda	(AUT)	1975		M Schumacher	(GER)	2002
	Ronnie Peterson	(SWE)	1973		Ayrton Senna	(BRA)	1985

IN ONE SEASON, CONSTRUCTORS

15	McLaren 1988		Williams 1987		Ferrari 2000
	McLaren 1989		Williams 1995		Ferrari 2002
	Williams 1992		Williams 1996		Lotus 1973
	Williams 1993	11	Ferrari 2001		McLaren 1991
12	Lotus 1978		McLaren 1999		Renault 1982
	McLaren 1990		Williams 1997	9	Brabham 1984
	McLaren 1998	10	Ferrari 1974		Ferrari 1975

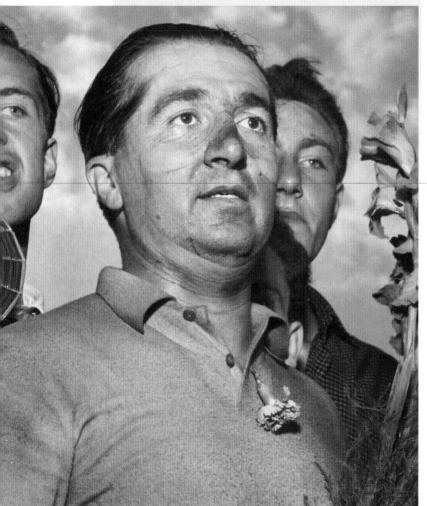

Looking To The Skies: Italian star Alberto Ascari set the fastest lap in every Grand Prix in 1952 as he dominated proceedings for Ferrari.

Unusual Order: Rubens Barrichello punches the air after reversing the usual Ferrari order at the Nurburgring in the 2002 European Grand Prix.

MOST POINTS

This figure is gross tally, i.e. including scores that were later dropped

DRIVERS

945	M Schumacher	(GER)	310	Carlos Reutemann	(ARG)
798.5	Alain Prost	(FRA)	289	Graham Hill	(GBR)
614	Ayrton Senna	(BRA)	281	Emerson Fittipaldi	(BRA)
485.5	Nelson Piquet	(BRA)		Riccardo Patrese	(ITA)
482	Nigel Mansell	(GBR)	277.5	Juan Manuel Fangio	(ARG)
420.5	Niki Lauda	(AUT)	274	Jim Clark	(GBR)
420	Mika Hakkinen	(FIN)	272	Rubens Barrichello	(BRA)
400	David Coulthard	(GBR)	261	Jack Brabham	(AUS)
385	Gerhard Berger	(AUT)	255	Jody Scheckter	(RSA)
360	Damon Hill	(GBR)	248	Denny Hulme	(NZL)
	Jackie Stewart	(GBR)	242	Jean Alesi	(FRA)

CONSTRUCTORS

2924.5	Ferrari	439	BRM	155	Matra
2647.5	McLaren	424	Prost	123	Sauber
2203.5	Williams	335	Renault	79	Wolf
1352	Lotus	333	Cooper	68	Jaguar
877.5	Benetton	259	Jordan	67.5	Shadow
854	Brabham	171.5	March	57	Vanwall
617	Tyrrell	167	Arrows	54	Surtees

MOST TITLES

DRIVERS

5	Juan Manuel Fangio	(ARG)		Giuseppe Farina	(ITA)
	Michael Schumacher	(GER)		Mike Hawthorn	(GBR)
4	Alain Prost	(FRA)		Damon Hill	(GBR)
3	Jack Brabham	(AUS)		Phil Hill	(USA)
	Niki Lauda	(AUT)		Denis Hulme	(NZL)
	Nelson Piquet	(BRA)		James Hunt	(GBR)
	Ayrton Senna	(BRA)		Alan Jones	(AUS)
	Jackie Stewart	(GBR)		Nigel Mansell	(GBR)
2	Alberto Ascari	(ITA)		Jochen Rindt	(AUT)
	Jim Clark	(GBR)		Keke Rosberg	(FIN)
	Emerson Fittipaldi	(BRA)		Jody Scheckter	(ZA)
	Mika Hakkinen	(FIN)		John Surtees	(GBR)
	Graham Hill	(GBR)		Jacques Villeneuve	(CDN)
1	Mario Andretti	(USA)			

CONSTRUCTORS

12	Ferrari	2	Brabham		Matra
9	Williams		Cooper		Tyrrell
8	McLaren	1	Benetton		Vanwall
7	Lotus		BRM		

2003 FIA FORMULA ONE

2003 FIA
FORMULA ONE
WORLD
CHAMPIONSHIP

	Driver	Car	March 9 AUSTRALIAN GP	March 23 MALAYSIAN GP	April 6 BRAZILIAN GP	April 20 SAN MARINO GP	May 4 SPANISH GP	May 18 AUSTRIAN GP	June 1 MONACO GP
1	MICHAEL SCHUMACHER	Ferrari							
2	RUBENS BARRICHELLO	Ferrari							
3	JUAN PABLO MONTOYA	Williams							
4	RALF SCHUMACHER	Williams							
5	DAVID COULTHARD	McLaren							
6	KIMI RAIKKONEN	McLaren							
7	JARNO TRULLI	Renault							
8	FERNANDO ALONSO	Renault							
9	NICK HEIDFELD	Sauber							
10	HEINZ-HARALD FRENTZEN	Sauber							
11	GIANCARLO FISICHELLA	Jordan							
12	tba	Jordan							
14	MARK WEBBER	Jaguar							
15	ANTONIO PIZZONIA	Jaguar							
16	JACQUES VILLENEUVE	BAR							
17	JENSON BUTTON	BAR							
18	JUSTIN WILSON	Minardi							
19	JOS VERSTAPPEN	Minardi							
20	OLIVIER PANIS	Toyota							
21	CRISTIANO DA MATTA	Toyota							

WORLD CHAMPIONSHIP ≫

June 15 **CANADIAN GP**	June 29 **EUROPEAN GP**	July 6 **FRENCH GP**	July 20 **BRITISH GP**	August 3 **GERMAN GP**	August 24 **HUNGARIAN GP**	September 14 **ITALIAN GP**	September 14 **UNITED STATES GP**	October 13 **JAPANESE GP**	Points Total

2003 FIA
FORMULA ONE
WORLD
CHAMPIONSHIP

Scoring system: 10, 8, 6, 5, 4, 3, 2, 1 for the first eight finishers.

Trophy Number Five: Michael Schumacher holds aloft his fifth Formula One drivers' trophy at last year's FIA Awards. What chance he lifts trophy number six in 2003?

The publishers would like to thank the following sources for their kind permission to reproduce the pictures in this book.

Getty Images: Robert Cianflone 32, 45, 104, Mike Cooper 68 Tony Feder 17, Mike Hewitt 105 Bryn Lennon 12, 13, 15, 18, 27, 86, 91, 93, 98, 101, 104, 111, Clive Mason 10, 16, 19, 20, 24, 29, 34, 40, 56, 57, 59, 60, 63, 65, 66, 74, 82, 94, 95, 100, 102, 103, 105, 109 Pascal Rondeau 43, 58, 69, 70 Tom Shaw 4, 14, 89, 92, 96, Mark Thompson 2, 3, 5 (both), 11, 21, 22, 23, 25, 26, 28, 30, 33, 38, 44, 57, 62, 64, 67, 71, 72, 73, 84, 85, 87, 88, 90, 97, 98, 99, 100, 101, 106, 107, 108, 109, 110 Ian Walton 36

Empics, Alpha 104, Jed Leicester 7, 8, 31, 66, Steve Mitchell 61

Corbis 42

Hulton Archive 108

Every effort has been made to acknowledge correctly and contact the source and/or copyright holder of each picture, and Carlton Books Ltd apologises for any unintentional errors or omissions which will be corrected in future editions.

Illustrations: Graphic News, Colin Bull, F1 Bahrain